Network Segmentation and Microsegmentation

James Relington

DEDICATION

To those who seek knowledge, inspiration, and new perspectives—
may this book be a companion on your journey, a spark for curiosity,
and a reminder that every page turned is a step toward discovery.

AKNOWLEDGEMENTS

I would like to express my deepest gratitude to everyone who contributed to the creation of this book. To my colleagues and mentors, your insights and expertise have been invaluable. A special thank you to my family and friends for their unwavering support and encouragement throughout this journey.

Introduction to Network Segmentation

Network segmentation is a fundamental cybersecurity strategy that involves dividing a network into smaller, isolated sections to improve security, performance, and manageability. As networks grow increasingly complex, segmentation becomes essential to mitigate risks, prevent unauthorized access, and control traffic flow. Organizations rely on segmentation to minimize the impact of security breaches, reduce lateral movement of threats, and ensure that only authorized users and systems can communicate with each other. By implementing network segmentation effectively, businesses can enhance their security posture and maintain compliance with industry regulations.

The concept of network segmentation has evolved significantly over the years, transitioning from traditional physical segmentation to modern logical segmentation techniques. In the past, organizations relied on separate physical networks, using dedicated hardware to create isolated environments. While effective, this approach was costly and difficult to scale. Today, advances in virtualization, software-defined networking, and cloud computing allow for more flexible and dynamic segmentation methods. Logical segmentation, which relies on policies and software controls rather than physical infrastructure, has become the preferred approach for most enterprises.

One of the primary benefits of network segmentation is the containment of security threats. In a flat, unsegmented network, an attacker who gains access to a single device can often move laterally and compromise additional systems without encountering significant obstacles. Segmentation limits this movement by enforcing strict access controls between different network segments. For example, an organization might separate its internal user network from its critical infrastructure, ensuring that even if an attacker infiltrates a workstation, they cannot easily reach sensitive servers or databases. This approach significantly reduces the potential damage of a cyberattack and provides additional layers of defense.

Beyond security, network segmentation also improves performance by optimizing traffic flow. In large networks with high volumes of data transmission, congestion can become a major issue, leading to slow response times and reduced efficiency. By segmenting the network, organizations can isolate high-traffic areas, ensuring that mission-critical applications receive the necessary bandwidth without interference from less important traffic. This is particularly beneficial in environments such as data centers, where multiple applications and services operate simultaneously. Segmentation enables IT teams to prioritize network resources, allocate bandwidth more effectively, and reduce overall network latency.

Compliance with industry regulations is another key driver for network segmentation. Many regulatory frameworks, such as the Payment Card Industry Data Security Standard (PCI DSS), the Health Insurance Portability and Accountability Act (HIPAA), and the General Data Protection Regulation (GDPR), require organizations to implement strict access controls and data protection measures. Network segmentation helps businesses meet these requirements by restricting access to sensitive information, logging network activity, and ensuring that only authorized personnel can interact with protected resources. Failure to implement proper segmentation can lead to compliance violations, resulting in fines, legal consequences, and reputational damage.

The implementation of network segmentation requires careful planning and consideration of an organization's infrastructure, security policies, and operational needs. One of the first steps in segmentation is identifying critical assets and determining which systems should be isolated from each other. This involves mapping network traffic, analyzing dependencies between applications, and defining access control policies based on the principle of least privilege. Organizations must also consider how segmentation will affect network management and ensure that segmentation policies are enforceable without introducing unnecessary complexity.

Modern network segmentation strategies often leverage technologies such as virtual local area networks (VLANs), access control lists (ACLs), and next-generation firewalls (NGFWs) to enforce boundaries between different segments. VLANs provide logical separation of network traffic, allowing administrators to group devices based on function rather than physical location. ACLs define rules for traffic filtering, specifying which devices can communicate with each other based on predefined criteria. Firewalls play a crucial role by inspecting and controlling traffic between segments, blocking unauthorized access attempts, and detecting potential threats in real time.

Microsegmentation is an advanced form of network segmentation that provides even greater control over traffic flow and access permissions. Unlike traditional segmentation, which typically operates at the subnet or VLAN level, microsegmentation applies security policies at the workload level. This means that even within a single subnet, individual applications, services, or virtual machines can be isolated from each other. Microsegmentation is particularly valuable in cloud environments, where traditional network boundaries are less defined, and workloads need granular security policies. By adopting microsegmentation, organizations can enforce strict security controls without relying solely on perimeter-based defenses.

Despite its benefits, network segmentation also presents challenges. Poorly implemented segmentation can lead to operational disruptions, increased complexity, and difficulties in troubleshooting network issues. Over-segmentation, where excessive restrictions are placed on communication between systems, can hinder business operations and create unnecessary administrative burdens. On the other hand, under-segmentation leaves networks vulnerable to attacks by failing to provide adequate isolation between critical assets. Striking the right balance requires a thorough understanding of network architecture, continuous monitoring of traffic patterns, and regular updates to segmentation policies to adapt to evolving threats.

The rise of cloud computing, hybrid IT environments, and the Internet of Things (IoT) has further complicated network segmentation. Organizations must now segment not only traditional on-premises infrastructure but also cloud-based resources, remote users, and connected devices. This shift has led to the adoption of software-defined segmentation, where network policies are dynamically applied based on real-time conditions rather than static configurations. Automation and artificial intelligence are playing an increasing role in managing segmentation, helping organizations detect anomalies, enforce policies efficiently, and respond to threats in a more proactive manner.

Network segmentation is a cornerstone of modern cybersecurity, providing organizations with a powerful tool to enhance security, improve performance, and achieve compliance. As threats continue to evolve, segmentation strategies must also adapt, incorporating new technologies and best practices to remain effective. By implementing network segmentation thoughtfully and continuously refining their approach, organizations can create a more resilient and secure network infrastructure, reducing the risk of cyberattacks and ensuring the integrity of their systems and data.

The Importance of Network Security

Network security is a critical component of modern digital infrastructure, ensuring the confidentiality, integrity, and availability of data and services. As organizations become more reliant on interconnected systems, the potential risks associated with cyber threats continue to grow. Cybercriminals, nation-state actors, and malicious insiders constantly seek vulnerabilities to exploit, making network security a necessity for businesses, governments, and individuals alike. Without robust security measures in place, networks remain vulnerable to attacks that can disrupt operations, compromise sensitive information, and result in significant financial and reputational damage.

One of the most pressing concerns in network security is the ever-expanding attack surface. With the proliferation of cloud computing, remote work, mobile devices, and Internet of Things (IoT) technologies, networks are more complex and dispersed than ever before. Each additional endpoint, application, and service introduces new potential entry points for attackers. Organizations must continuously adapt their security strategies to account for these evolving threats, implementing layers of defense to detect and mitigate attacks before they cause harm. Failure to address these risks can lead to devastating consequences, including data breaches, identity theft, and operational downtime.

The financial impact of network security breaches can be staggering. Companies that suffer cyberattacks often face immediate financial losses from theft, fraud, and ransom demands. Additionally, regulatory fines and legal consequences can add to the burden, especially for businesses that handle sensitive customer data. The cost of recovering from an attack extends beyond immediate monetary losses, as organizations must invest in forensic investigations, incident response efforts, and long-term security enhancements to prevent future incidents. Reputation damage is another major concern, as customers and partners may lose trust in an organization that fails to protect its data.

Network security is also crucial for maintaining compliance with regulatory requirements. Many industries are subject to strict cybersecurity laws and standards designed to protect sensitive information. Regulations such as the General Data Protection Regulation (GDPR), the Health Insurance Portability and Accountability Act (HIPAA), and the Payment Card Industry Data Security Standard (PCI DSS) require organizations to implement strong security controls to safeguard personal and financial data. Noncompliance can result in severe penalties, including hefty fines and legal action. By prioritizing network security, businesses can ensure compliance with these regulations while minimizing the risk of legal exposure.

Cyber threats are constantly evolving, making it essential for organizations to stay ahead of attackers. Traditional security measures, such as firewalls and antivirus software, are no longer sufficient on their own. Cybercriminals use sophisticated techniques, including social engineering, zero-day exploits, and advanced persistent threats (APTs), to bypass traditional defenses. Phishing attacks remain one of the most common and effective methods used by attackers to gain access to networks. Employees are often the weakest link in security, as they may unknowingly click on malicious links or disclose sensitive information. Security awareness training and strong authentication mechanisms play a vital role in mitigating these risks.

The adoption of a layered security approach, also known as defense in depth, is one of the most effective ways to protect networks. This strategy involves implementing multiple security controls at different levels of the network to create redundancies and prevent single points of failure. Firewalls, intrusion detection and prevention systems, endpoint security solutions, and encryption technologies all contribute to a comprehensive security posture. Network segmentation further enhances security by limiting the movement of attackers within a network, reducing the potential damage of a breach. By combining these measures, organizations can build a resilient security framework that can withstand modern cyber threats.

Cloud security has become a growing concern as more businesses migrate their operations to cloud environments. While cloud computing offers numerous benefits, including scalability, cost savings, and flexibility, it also introduces new security challenges. Organizations must ensure that their cloud providers adhere to strict security standards and implement strong access controls to protect cloud-based assets. Misconfigurations are one of the leading causes of cloud security breaches, often exposing sensitive data to unauthorized users. Regular security assessments, continuous monitoring, and encryption of cloud data are essential to mitigate these risks.

Remote work has further emphasized the importance of network security, as employees connect to corporate networks from various locations and devices. The shift to remote work has increased the use of virtual private networks (VPNs), multi-factor authentication (MFA), and endpoint detection and response (EDR) solutions to secure remote access. However, attackers have also adapted their tactics, targeting remote workers with phishing campaigns, credential stuffing attacks, and ransomware. Organizations must enforce strict security policies for remote employees, ensuring that only authorized users and devices can access sensitive corporate resources.

Insider threats pose a significant risk to network security, as malicious or negligent employees can expose an organization to cyberattacks. Insider threats can take many forms, including data theft, unauthorized access, and sabotage. Unlike external threats, which originate from outside the network, insider threats come from within and can be harder to detect. Implementing strict access controls, monitoring user behavior, and employing data loss prevention (DLP) tools can help mitigate the risks associated with insider threats. Organizations should also foster a culture of security awareness, ensuring that employees understand their role in protecting the network.

The rise of artificial intelligence (AI) and machine learning (ML) has both positive and negative implications for network security. On one hand, AI-powered security solutions can analyze vast amounts of data in real time, identifying anomalies and potential threats more efficiently than traditional methods. Machine learning algorithms can detect patterns indicative of cyberattacks, enabling faster and more effective incident response. On the other hand, cybercriminals are also leveraging AI to develop more sophisticated attack techniques, automating phishing campaigns and evading traditional security measures. Organizations must stay ahead by integrating AI-driven security solutions while remaining vigilant against emerging threats.

Threat intelligence plays a crucial role in enhancing network security by providing organizations with valuable insights into the latest cyber threats. By collecting and analyzing threat data from various sources, security teams can proactively identify vulnerabilities and take preventive measures before an attack occurs. Sharing threat intelligence within industry groups and cybersecurity communities can also strengthen collective defenses, as organizations collaborate to combat common threats. Security teams must stay informed about the latest attack trends, vulnerabilities, and tactics used by cybercriminals to continuously refine their security strategies.

The importance of network security cannot be overstated, as it serves as the foundation for protecting digital assets, maintaining business continuity, and safeguarding sensitive information. Cyber threats will continue to evolve, making it imperative for organizations to adopt a proactive approach to security. By implementing comprehensive security measures, staying informed about emerging threats, and fostering a security-conscious culture, businesses can reduce their risk exposure and strengthen their overall cybersecurity posture.

Traditional vs. Modern Segmentation Approaches

Network segmentation has long been a fundamental strategy for securing and managing network environments. Over time, approaches to segmentation have evolved significantly to keep pace with technological advancements, new security challenges, and the increasing complexity of modern IT infrastructures. Traditional segmentation methods relied primarily on physical barriers and rudimentary access controls, whereas modern segmentation leverages advanced software-defined techniques, automation, and granular policy enforcement to create more effective and dynamic security perimeters. Understanding the differences between these approaches is crucial for organizations looking to implement a robust network segmentation strategy that aligns with contemporary security needs.

Traditional network segmentation was largely based on physical infrastructure, where networks were divided using dedicated hardware devices such as routers, switches, and firewalls. This approach created isolated network segments, often separated by department, function, or security level. Organizations would physically segment different areas of their network by using separate network cables, dedicated subnets, and distinct network appliances. While effective at enforcing basic access controls and minimizing traffic congestion, this method was inflexible, expensive, and difficult to scale. Any changes to the network structure required manual configuration of hardware devices, leading to increased administrative overhead and a lack of adaptability in dynamic environments.

VLANs, or Virtual Local Area Networks, became a widely adopted technique in traditional segmentation, allowing organizations to logically separate network traffic without requiring extensive physical infrastructure changes. VLANs provided greater flexibility by enabling administrators to segment networks based on logical groupings rather than physical location. However, VLAN-based segmentation still required significant manual configuration, and improper implementation often led to security vulnerabilities. Attackers could exploit misconfigured VLANs, VLAN hopping attacks, and insufficient access controls to move laterally across the network. Despite these challenges, VLANs remained a standard method for network segmentation in traditional environments.

Firewalls played a central role in traditional segmentation by acting as the primary enforcement point between network segments. Organizations deployed firewalls to control traffic between different segments, defining rules that specified which traffic was allowed or denied based on source, destination, and protocol. While firewalls provided a reasonable level of security, they were often deployed at the perimeter of network segments rather than at a granular level. This meant that once an attacker breached a segment, they could move laterally with minimal restrictions, especially in networks with broad trust relationships between internal devices. Traditional segmentation was therefore limited in its ability to prevent lateral movement and isolate threats effectively.

As network environments evolved, the limitations of traditional segmentation became more apparent. The rise of cloud computing, virtualization, remote work, and IoT devices introduced new challenges that traditional approaches struggled to address. Static, hardware-based segmentation could not keep up with the dynamic nature of modern IT infrastructures, where workloads move between on-premises data centers and cloud environments, and users access resources from various locations and devices. The increasing sophistication of cyber threats further highlighted the need for a more adaptive and granular segmentation approach that could provide real-time enforcement of security policies across distributed environments.

Modern segmentation, often referred to as software-defined segmentation or microsegmentation, represents a significant evolution in how organizations secure their networks. Unlike traditional methods that rely on physical infrastructure, modern segmentation leverages software-defined networking (SDN), identity-based controls, and automation to enforce security policies at a much finer level. This approach allows organizations to create highly granular segmentation rules that define how workloads, users, and devices communicate within a network, regardless of their physical location. Instead of relying on broad network perimeters, modern segmentation focuses on securing individual applications, workloads, and data flows.

One of the key technologies driving modern segmentation is microsegmentation. Unlike VLAN-based segmentation, which operates at the network layer, microsegmentation applies security controls at the workload or application level. This means that even within the same subnet or virtualized environment, individual workloads can be isolated from each other, preventing unauthorized communication. Microsegmentation is particularly valuable in cloud and hybrid environments, where traditional segmentation methods cannot provide sufficient security granularity. By enforcing policies based on workload identities, rather than static network parameters, organizations can significantly reduce the risk of lateral movement and insider threats.

Another critical aspect of modern segmentation is dynamic policy enforcement. Traditional segmentation required manual rule creation and updates, which often led to misconfigurations and security gaps. Modern segmentation solutions leverage automation, artificial intelligence, and machine learning to dynamically adapt security policies based on real-time network activity and threat intelligence. This enables organizations to respond more quickly to evolving threats, automatically adjusting segmentation rules to contain potential breaches. By integrating with security analytics and monitoring tools, modern segmentation can provide continuous visibility into network traffic patterns, helping organizations detect and mitigate security risks more effectively.

Identity-based segmentation is another advancement that differentiates modern segmentation from traditional approaches. Instead of relying solely on IP addresses and network topology, identity-based segmentation assigns security policies based on user roles, device attributes, and authentication status. This ensures that access control is enforced consistently across all environments, regardless of where users or devices connect from. With the adoption of Zero Trust security models, identity-based segmentation has become a crucial component of protecting modern networks, as it ensures that only authenticated and authorized entities can access specific resources.

Cloud-native segmentation further extends modern segmentation capabilities by providing security controls tailored for cloud environments. Unlike traditional segmentation, which was designed for on-premises data centers, cloud-native segmentation enables organizations to apply security policies across multi-cloud and hybrid cloud infrastructures. Cloud providers offer built-in segmentation features such as security groups, network access control lists (NACLs), and service meshes that allow organizations to enforce access control between cloud workloads. By combining cloud-native security controls with microsegmentation and automation, organizations can achieve a consistent and scalable security posture across diverse environments.

The shift from traditional to modern segmentation is driven by the need for greater security agility, reduced operational complexity, and improved threat containment. Traditional segmentation methods, while still relevant in certain scenarios, are no longer sufficient to address the challenges posed by today's dynamic IT environments. Modern segmentation provides organizations with the flexibility to secure their networks at a granular level, enabling them to protect sensitive data, mitigate cyber threats, and ensure compliance with regulatory requirements. As cyberattacks become more sophisticated and networks continue to evolve, adopting modern segmentation approaches is essential for building a resilient and secure digital infrastructure.

Understanding Network Architectures

Network architectures form the foundation of modern digital communication, enabling organizations to connect devices, applications, and users while ensuring efficient data transmission, security, and scalability. A well-designed network architecture provides structure, defines communication pathways, and establishes security controls that govern how data moves across an organization's infrastructure. Understanding network architectures is essential for IT professionals, security teams, and business leaders seeking to optimize performance, enhance cybersecurity, and support emerging technologies such as cloud computing, the Internet of Things, and artificial intelligence.

At its core, network architecture refers to the design and framework of a network, including its topology, components, and communication protocols. Traditional network architectures followed a hierarchical model, consisting of core, distribution, and access layers. The core layer acts as the backbone of the network, facilitating high-speed data transfer between different sections. The distribution layer manages traffic flow and enforces policies, ensuring security and efficient routing of data. The access layer connects end-user devices, including computers, phones, and IoT devices, to the network. This layered approach has long been a standard for enterprise networks, providing a structured method for managing connectivity and security.

Advancements in technology have introduced more flexible and scalable network architectures that depart from traditional hierarchical models. Software-defined networking, cloud-based architectures, and edge computing have transformed how networks are designed and operated. Software-defined networking decouples the control plane from the data plane, allowing network administrators to manage traffic programmatically rather than through hardware-based configurations. This flexibility enables rapid adjustments, automation, and improved security by enforcing policies at a granular level. By centralizing control, organizations can respond to threats more effectively, reduce complexity, and scale their networks with minimal manual intervention.

Cloud-based architectures have significantly altered how businesses deploy and manage network infrastructure. In traditional on-premises networks, organizations maintain physical servers, switches, and routers within their data centers. Cloud networking shifts many of these functions to cloud service providers, allowing organizations to access scalable computing resources without the burden of managing physical infrastructure. Hybrid cloud architectures blend on-premises and cloud environments, enabling businesses to retain critical workloads in their private data centers while leveraging the scalability and flexibility of public cloud services. This hybrid approach provides organizations with greater agility, allowing them to optimize costs, improve resilience, and maintain control over sensitive data.

The increasing reliance on edge computing has introduced additional complexities in network architecture design. Unlike centralized cloud computing, which processes data in remote data centers, edge computing brings processing power closer to the source of data generation. This is particularly important for applications that require low latency, such as autonomous vehicles, industrial automation, and real-time analytics. By distributing computing resources at the network edge, organizations can reduce reliance on centralized cloud infrastructure while enhancing performance and responsiveness. Edge computing requires a reimagining of network architecture, as data must be securely transmitted, processed, and analyzed at various locations without compromising security or efficiency.

Security plays a critical role in network architecture, influencing how data flows and how access is controlled. Traditional perimeter-based security models focused on defending the network's outer boundaries using firewalls and intrusion prevention systems. However, as cyber threats have evolved and organizations have adopted cloud computing and remote work, perimeter security alone is no longer sufficient. Zero Trust Architecture has emerged as a modern approach to network security, operating on the principle that no entity—internal or external—should be automatically trusted. In a Zero Trust model, access is granted based on identity verification, contextual factors, and strict policy enforcement, reducing the risk of unauthorized access and lateral movement within the network.

Network segmentation is an essential component of secure network architectures. By dividing a network into smaller, isolated segments, organizations can limit the spread of cyber threats and enforce access controls based on role, function, or sensitivity of data. Traditional network segmentation relied on VLANs and firewall rules, while modern approaches use microsegmentation to enforce security policies at the workload level. Microsegmentation allows organizations to define granular security policies for individual applications, servers, and services, reducing the attack surface and mitigating the impact of breaches. This level of control is particularly important in cloud and hybrid environments, where dynamic workloads require flexible security enforcement.

Network architectures must also consider redundancy and fault tolerance to ensure high availability and resilience. Downtime can result in significant financial losses and reputational damage, making it crucial for organizations to design networks that can withstand failures and disruptions. Redundant connections, load balancing, and failover mechanisms help maintain network availability in the event of hardware failures, cyberattacks, or natural disasters. High-availability architectures use multiple data centers, distributed networks, and automated failover solutions to minimize disruptions and ensure continuous service delivery. By implementing robust redundancy strategies, organizations can enhance reliability and prevent single points of failure from compromising their operations.

The rapid growth of IoT devices has further complicated network architecture, requiring organizations to address scalability, security, and management challenges. Unlike traditional IT assets, IoT devices often operate in diverse environments, from manufacturing plants to smart cities, and have varying levels of security capabilities. Network architectures must accommodate these devices while implementing stringent security controls to prevent unauthorized access and data breaches. Segmentation, endpoint security, and anomaly detection are essential components of IoT network security, helping organizations monitor device activity, enforce policies, and mitigate potential threats. As the number of connected devices continues to rise, network architectures must evolve to handle the increased traffic, complexity, and security risks.

Artificial intelligence and machine learning are playing an increasingly important role in network architecture optimization and security. AI-driven analytics can monitor network traffic, detect anomalies, and predict potential failures before they occur. Machine learning algorithms can analyze vast amounts of data in real time, identifying patterns that indicate cyber threats or performance issues. AI-powered network management solutions enable automated responses to security incidents, reducing the need for manual intervention and improving overall efficiency. By integrating AI into network architecture, organizations can enhance threat detection, streamline operations, and improve resilience against evolving cyber threats.

Network architectures must continuously evolve to meet the demands of modern digital environments. The shift from traditional hierarchical models to software-defined, cloud-based, and edge computing architectures reflects the changing nature of IT infrastructure and security requirements. Organizations must design networks that prioritize flexibility, security, and scalability while addressing the complexities introduced by remote work, IoT, and AI-driven automation. By understanding the principles of network architecture and adopting modern design strategies, businesses can build resilient and efficient networks capable of supporting future technological advancements.

Key Concepts in Network Segmentation

Network segmentation is a foundational security and performance optimization strategy that involves dividing a network into smaller, isolated segments to control traffic flow and enforce access restrictions. As cyber threats continue to evolve, organizations rely on segmentation to reduce attack surfaces, limit unauthorized access, and improve overall network efficiency. By implementing effective segmentation strategies, organizations can create secure environments that minimize the risk of data breaches, mitigate lateral movement of threats, and ensure compliance with industry regulations. Understanding the key concepts behind network segmentation is essential for designing and maintaining a secure and resilient IT infrastructure.

One of the fundamental principles of network segmentation is the separation of network traffic based on business function, security level, or data sensitivity. Organizations often divide networks into distinct zones, each with its own access controls and security policies. For example, a corporate network may consist of segments for employee workstations, internal servers, guest Wi-Fi, and cloud-based applications. By isolating these segments, organizations can prevent unauthorized access between different parts of the network and reduce the impact of potential cyberattacks. This approach ensures that even if an attacker gains access to one segment, they cannot easily move laterally to more sensitive areas.

Traffic control and enforcement mechanisms play a crucial role in network segmentation. Firewalls, access control lists (ACLs), and intrusion prevention systems (IPS) are commonly used to regulate communication between network segments. Firewalls define rules that allow or deny traffic based on predefined criteria such as source IP address, destination IP address, protocol, and port number. ACLs function as filters that enforce access restrictions by specifying which devices or users can communicate with each other. Intrusion prevention systems provide an additional layer of security by monitoring traffic patterns and blocking suspicious activity that may indicate a cyber threat.

Virtual Local Area Networks (VLANs) are a widely used method of network segmentation that enables logical separation of devices within a network. VLANs allow administrators to group devices based on department, function, or access requirements without requiring physical separation. By assigning devices to VLANs, organizations can isolate traffic and enforce security policies without adding additional hardware. VLAN tagging ensures that traffic remains within its designated segment, preventing unauthorized access between different groups. While VLANs offer flexibility and scalability, misconfigurations can introduce security risks such as VLAN hopping, where attackers exploit vulnerabilities to bypass segmentation controls.

Microsegmentation is an advanced segmentation technique that provides granular control over network traffic by enforcing security policies at the workload or application level. Unlike traditional segmentation, which operates at the subnet or VLAN level, microsegmentation allows organizations to define access policies for individual applications, virtual machines, or containers. This approach is particularly valuable in cloud environments, where workloads are dynamic and distributed across multiple locations. Microsegmentation ensures that only authorized entities can communicate with specific resources, reducing the risk of insider threats and unauthorized lateral movement. Security policies in microsegmentation are typically enforced using software-defined networking (SDN) technologies, enabling automated policy management and real-time adaptation to changing network conditions.

The principle of least privilege (PoLP) is a core concept in network segmentation that dictates that users, applications, and devices should only have the minimum level of access required to perform their functions. By restricting access to only necessary resources, organizations can limit the potential damage of security breaches and insider threats. Implementing least privilege requires careful analysis of access requirements, continuous monitoring of user behavior, and regular audits to ensure compliance with security policies. Role-based access control (RBAC) and attribute-based access control (ABAC) are commonly used to enforce least privilege in segmented networks, granting access based on predefined roles, user attributes, or contextual factors such as location and device type.

Zero Trust Architecture (ZTA) aligns closely with network segmentation by emphasizing continuous verification and strict access controls. In a Zero Trust model, no entity—whether inside or outside the network—is automatically trusted. Access is granted based on identity authentication, device compliance, and contextual factors such as time of access and geolocation. Network segmentation supports Zero Trust by enforcing boundaries that prevent unauthorized movement between segments. By implementing microsegmentation and identity-based policies, organizations can create a Zero Trust environment where access decisions are dynamic and continuously assessed based on risk levels.

Network visibility and monitoring are essential for maintaining effective segmentation. Without proper visibility, organizations cannot ensure that segmentation policies are being enforced correctly or detect potential security breaches. Security Information and Event Management (SIEM) systems, network traffic analysis tools, and endpoint detection and response (EDR) solutions provide insights into network activity, enabling real-time threat detection and response. Network segmentation logs should be regularly reviewed to identify anomalies, unauthorized access attempts, and misconfigurations that could weaken security controls. Continuous monitoring ensures that segmentation remains effective and adapts to evolving security threats.

Compliance and regulatory requirements play a significant role in shaping network segmentation strategies. Many industries are subject to regulations that mandate strict access controls and data protection measures. The Payment Card Industry Data Security Standard (PCI DSS) requires organizations handling credit card transactions to segment their networks to isolate cardholder data from other systems.

The Health Insurance Portability and Accountability Act (HIPAA) mandates segmentation of healthcare networks to protect patient information. The General Data Protection Regulation (GDPR) emphasizes data protection by design, which includes network segmentation as a means of safeguarding personal data. Organizations must align their segmentation practices with regulatory requirements to avoid legal and financial penalties.

Automation and orchestration have become increasingly important in network segmentation, allowing organizations to manage segmentation policies efficiently and at scale. Traditional segmentation methods relied on manual configuration, which was time-consuming and prone to human error. Modern segmentation solutions leverage automation to enforce policies dynamically, based on real-time network activity and threat intelligence. Security orchestration platforms integrate with firewalls, SDN controllers, and identity management systems to apply segmentation rules consistently across cloud, on-premises, and hybrid environments. By automating segmentation, organizations can reduce complexity, improve response times to security incidents, and ensure that segmentation policies remain up to date.

The effectiveness of network segmentation depends on proper implementation, continuous monitoring, and alignment with security best practices. Organizations must conduct regular risk assessments to identify critical assets, define segmentation boundaries, and evaluate potential attack vectors. Security teams should work closely with network administrators to design segmentation policies that balance security with operational efficiency. By adopting a proactive approach to segmentation, organizations can create a secure and resilient network infrastructure that protects against cyber threats, optimizes performance, and supports business continuity.

Microsegmentation: A Deeper Dive

Microsegmentation is an advanced network security strategy that provides highly granular control over traffic flows, restricting communication between workloads, applications, and devices based on predefined policies. Unlike traditional network segmentation, which operates at the subnet or VLAN level, microsegmentation enforces security policies at a much finer level, ensuring that even individual workloads within the same network segment remain isolated from each other unless explicitly authorized to communicate. This approach minimizes the attack surface, prevents lateral movement by cyber threats, and enhances overall security posture by ensuring that access to resources is strictly controlled.

The growing adoption of cloud computing, virtualization, and distributed workloads has made traditional segmentation methods insufficient for modern IT environments. In traditional networks, segmentation was primarily achieved through firewalls, access control lists, and VLANs, but these methods lack the flexibility and granularity needed to secure dynamic workloads. Microsegmentation addresses this limitation by decoupling security policies from network topology and applying them based on workload identities, user attributes, and behavioral context. This identity-based approach enables organizations to create highly adaptive security models that evolve alongside their infrastructure without requiring constant manual reconfiguration.

One of the primary advantages of microsegmentation is its ability to prevent unauthorized lateral movement within a network. In traditional flat networks, once an attacker gains access to a single system, they can move freely across the network, searching for valuable data or vulnerable systems to exploit. This type of attack, known as lateral movement, is commonly used in ransomware campaigns and advanced persistent threats. Microsegmentation blocks such movement by restricting communication between workloads to only what is explicitly necessary for business functions. Even if an attacker breaches one workload, they will be unable to pivot to other systems without triggering security alerts or encountering access restrictions.

Policy enforcement in microsegmentation is typically implemented using software-defined security controls rather than relying on physical network infrastructure. These controls are enforced at the workload level, using host-based firewalls, identity-based rules, or software-defined networking (SDN) policies. Organizations can define security policies based on factors such as application type, user role, device identity, or real-time behavioral analysis. Unlike static firewall rules, which require manual configuration updates whenever network changes occur, microsegmentation policies are dynamic and automatically adapt to infrastructure changes. This level of automation reduces administrative overhead while ensuring continuous security enforcement.

Cloud environments benefit significantly from microsegmentation due to their highly dynamic and distributed nature. In multi-cloud and hybrid cloud environments, workloads frequently move between on-premises data centers and cloud providers, making traditional perimeter-based security models ineffective. Microsegmentation allows organizations to apply consistent security policies across cloud and on-premises workloads, ensuring that applications remain protected regardless of their location. Cloud-native security solutions leverage microsegmentation to enforce workload isolation, preventing unauthorized interactions between virtual machines, containers, and cloud-native services. By integrating microsegmentation with cloud security frameworks, organizations can achieve greater control over data flows and application communications.

Zero Trust principles align closely with microsegmentation by enforcing strict access controls and assuming that no entity should be trusted by default, regardless of whether it is inside or outside the network perimeter. A Zero Trust security model requires continuous verification of user identities, device security posture, and application behavior before granting access to network resources. Microsegmentation plays a crucial role in Zero Trust implementation by enforcing least-privilege access policies at a granular level. Instead of relying on broad network-based trust models, microsegmentation ensures that only explicitly authorized interactions are permitted, reducing the risk of unauthorized access and data breaches.

Microsegmentation also enhances regulatory compliance by ensuring that sensitive data remains protected within defined security boundaries. Many industry regulations, including GDPR, HIPAA, and PCI DSS, require organizations to implement strict access controls to protect personal and financial data. By segmenting workloads based on regulatory requirements, organizations can enforce data access restrictions, monitor compliance violations, and generate audit logs that demonstrate adherence to security policies. The ability to enforce workload-level segmentation helps businesses avoid compliance fines, legal repercussions, and reputational damage associated with data breaches.

One of the challenges in implementing microsegmentation is defining appropriate security policies without disrupting legitimate business operations. Overly restrictive policies can hinder application performance, delay workflows, and create operational inefficiencies. Organizations must conduct thorough network traffic analysis to understand communication patterns and identify necessary dependencies between workloads. Security teams should work closely with application owners to establish segmentation policies that balance security with usability. Continuous monitoring and policy refinement are essential to ensuring that microsegmentation remains effective without causing unnecessary complexity.

Automated policy generation and artificial intelligence-driven security analytics help simplify microsegmentation deployment by identifying optimal segmentation rules based on real-time network behavior. Machine learning algorithms can analyze historical traffic patterns, detect anomalies, and suggest policy adjustments to minimize attack surfaces without disrupting legitimate activities. AI-driven segmentation tools enhance visibility into network interactions, allowing security teams to detect unauthorized access attempts, policy violations, and potential cyber threats. By leveraging AI and automation, organizations can accelerate microsegmentation implementation and maintain a proactive security posture.

Microsegmentation deployment can be achieved through various technical approaches, including host-based firewalls, SDN controllers, and network security platforms. Host-based firewalls enforce security policies at the individual workload level, ensuring that only authorized connections are allowed. SDN controllers provide centralized policy management, enabling dynamic segmentation across distributed environments. Network security platforms integrate microsegmentation with existing security tools, allowing seamless policy enforcement across on-premises, cloud, and hybrid environments. The choice of microsegmentation approach depends on the organization's infrastructure, security requirements, and operational constraints.

Visibility is a crucial factor in the success of microsegmentation strategies. Without comprehensive visibility into network traffic, organizations may struggle to identify security gaps and enforce effective segmentation policies. Network traffic monitoring, flow analysis, and threat intelligence integration provide valuable insights into how workloads interact, helping security teams refine policies and detect potential risks. Continuous security assessments, penetration testing, and compliance audits further enhance the effectiveness of microsegmentation by validating its ability to prevent unauthorized access and contain cyber threats.

As organizations increasingly adopt cloud computing, IoT, and remote work models, the need for microsegmentation continues to grow. Traditional network security approaches are no longer sufficient to protect modern IT environments, where workloads are highly distributed and perimeter defenses are less effective. Microsegmentation offers a proactive security model that isolates threats, enforces least-privilege access, and ensures continuous compliance with regulatory requirements. By embracing microsegmentation, businesses can build resilient security architectures that protect critical assets from evolving cyber threats while maintaining operational efficiency and scalability.

Benefits of Network Segmentation

Network segmentation is a critical strategy for improving security, optimizing network performance, and ensuring regulatory compliance. By dividing a network into smaller, isolated segments, organizations can control access, reduce the attack surface, and improve overall network efficiency. As cyber threats continue to evolve, network segmentation has become an essential component of modern IT security, providing businesses with a robust defense against cyberattacks, minimizing the impact of breaches, and ensuring secure communication between different parts of the network.

One of the most significant benefits of network segmentation is its ability to prevent unauthorized lateral movement within a network. In a flat network architecture, an attacker who gains access to a single system can move freely across the entire network, searching for valuable assets, exploiting vulnerabilities, and escalating privileges. Segmentation disrupts this movement by creating barriers that limit the attacker's ability to traverse the network. By isolating sensitive systems from general user networks, organizations can contain breaches and prevent cybercriminals from accessing critical data and infrastructure.

Reducing the attack surface is another major advantage of network segmentation. In an unsegmented network, all systems are exposed to potential threats, increasing the likelihood of a successful cyberattack. By dividing the network into controlled segments, organizations can limit exposure and ensure that only essential communication is permitted between different parts of the network. This minimizes the number of entry points available to attackers, making it significantly harder for them to exploit vulnerabilities. A well-implemented segmentation strategy helps organizations create a more resilient security posture by restricting access to sensitive assets and enforcing strict communication policies.

Improved network performance is another key benefit of segmentation. Without proper segmentation, network congestion can become a major issue, particularly in large enterprises with high volumes of traffic. When all devices and applications share the same network segment, data packets compete for bandwidth, leading to slow response times, latency issues, and decreased efficiency. By segmenting the network, organizations can optimize traffic flow, ensuring that critical applications receive the necessary resources while preventing non-essential traffic from affecting performance. This is particularly important in data centers, where multiple applications, virtual machines, and services require uninterrupted connectivity.

Segmentation also plays a crucial role in securing Internet of Things (IoT) devices, which are increasingly being integrated into corporate networks. IoT devices often lack robust security features, making them attractive targets for cybercriminals. If these devices are connected to an unsegmented network, a single compromised IoT device can serve as a gateway for attackers to access other systems. By segmenting IoT devices into their own dedicated network, organizations can isolate them from critical business applications, reducing the risk of security breaches while maintaining proper control over device communications. This approach ensures that even if an IoT device is compromised, the damage remains contained within its designated segment.

Compliance with regulatory requirements is another significant advantage of network segmentation. Many industries are subject to strict cybersecurity regulations that mandate the protection of sensitive data through access controls and security policies. Regulations such as the General Data Protection Regulation (GDPR), the Payment Card Industry Data Security Standard (PCI DSS), and the Health Insurance Portability and Accountability Act (HIPAA) require organizations to implement measures that safeguard sensitive information. Network segmentation helps organizations meet these regulatory requirements by isolating sensitive data, restricting access to authorized users, and logging network activity for auditing purposes. Organizations that fail to implement segmentation risk facing regulatory fines, legal penalties, and reputational damage due to non-compliance.

By implementing network segmentation, organizations can also enhance their incident response capabilities. When a security breach occurs, segmented networks make it easier to identify and contain the threat. Security teams can isolate compromised segments, preventing the attack from spreading to other areas of the network. This allows organizations to respond quickly to incidents, minimizing downtime and reducing the overall impact of a cyberattack. Segmentation also improves forensic investigations by providing clearer network boundaries, enabling analysts to trace the origin of an attack and determine the extent of the damage more efficiently.

Protecting critical business applications is another important benefit of network segmentation. Organizations rely on a wide range of applications for daily operations, including customer relationship management (CRM) systems, enterprise resource planning (ERP) software, and cloud-based collaboration tools. If these applications are exposed to unnecessary network traffic or unauthorized access, they become vulnerable to cyber threats. By segmenting business-critical applications into isolated environments, organizations can enforce strict access controls, ensuring that only authorized users and systems can interact with these applications. This reduces the risk of application-based attacks and protects sensitive business data from unauthorized access.

The rise of hybrid cloud environments has made network segmentation even more essential. Many organizations operate across multiple cloud providers and on-premises infrastructure, creating complex network environments with diverse security requirements. Traditional perimeter-based security models are no longer sufficient to protect modern hybrid environments, as workloads frequently move between cloud and on-premises systems. Network segmentation enables organizations to enforce consistent security policies across hybrid environments, ensuring that workloads remain protected regardless of their location. By segmenting cloud resources, organizations can prevent unauthorized access, secure data transfers, and maintain control over cloud-based assets.

Microsegmentation, an advanced form of network segmentation, takes security to an even higher level by enforcing granular access controls at the workload level. Unlike traditional segmentation, which typically divides networks at the subnet or VLAN level, microsegmentation allows organizations to define security policies for individual applications, services, or virtual machines. This approach ensures that even within a single network segment, workloads remain isolated from each other unless explicitly authorized to communicate. Microsegmentation is particularly beneficial for securing dynamic cloud environments, where workloads frequently scale up or down based on demand. By implementing microsegmentation, organizations can achieve fine-grained control over network security while minimizing the risk of lateral movement by attackers.

Organizations that embrace network segmentation also benefit from enhanced security visibility and monitoring capabilities. By dividing the network into smaller segments, security teams gain greater visibility into network traffic patterns, making it easier to detect anomalies, unauthorized access attempts, and potential threats. Security Information and Event Management (SIEM) systems, network traffic analysis tools, and threat intelligence platforms can integrate with segmentation policies to provide real-time insights into network activity. This improved visibility allows organizations to proactively identify and mitigate security risks before they escalate into full-scale cyber incidents.

The adoption of Zero Trust security models further amplifies the importance of network segmentation. In a Zero Trust environment, no user or device is automatically trusted, and access is granted based on continuous verification. Network segmentation aligns with Zero Trust principles by ensuring that access controls are enforced at multiple levels, preventing unauthorized movement within the network. By integrating segmentation with identity-based security policies, organizations can create a highly secure architecture where access decisions are based on contextual factors such as user identity, device health, and real-time risk assessment.

As cyber threats continue to evolve, organizations must prioritize network segmentation as a fundamental security measure. By reducing attack surfaces, preventing lateral movement, optimizing network performance, ensuring regulatory compliance, and enhancing incident response capabilities, network segmentation provides a comprehensive approach to network security. Whether implemented through traditional segmentation methods or advanced microsegmentation techniques, the benefits of network segmentation make it a critical component of modern cybersecurity strategies. Organizations that invest in segmentation will be better equipped to protect their assets, maintain business continuity, and mitigate the risks associated with an increasingly complex and interconnected digital landscape.

Common Challenges in Network Segmentation

Network segmentation is a powerful security strategy that helps organizations isolate sensitive systems, reduce attack surfaces, and prevent unauthorized lateral movement. While the benefits of segmentation are well-documented, implementing and maintaining an effective segmentation strategy comes with significant challenges. Organizations often struggle with complexity, misconfigurations, performance trade-offs, and evolving security threats that can undermine the effectiveness of segmentation policies. Understanding these challenges is crucial for developing a robust segmentation framework that enhances security without disrupting business operations.

One of the most significant challenges in network segmentation is the complexity of implementation. Many organizations operate large, intricate networks that span multiple locations, cloud environments, and legacy systems. Segmentation requires careful planning and a deep understanding of how different network components interact. Without a clear roadmap, organizations may struggle to define proper segmentation boundaries, leading to inconsistencies that weaken security. Misalignment between security teams and network administrators can further complicate implementation, as segmentation policies must balance security requirements with operational needs. The lack of standardized segmentation frameworks can also make it difficult for organizations to adopt a consistent approach across different environments.

Misconfigurations pose a major risk in network segmentation, often resulting in unintended security gaps or operational disruptions. A poorly configured segmentation policy can either allow excessive access, defeating the purpose of segmentation, or restrict access too aggressively, causing legitimate applications and services to fail. Organizations frequently encounter issues where firewall rules, access control lists (ACLs), and VLAN settings conflict with one another, leading to unpredictable network behavior. Manually managing thousands of segmentation rules across different network devices increases the likelihood of human error. These misconfigurations can create hidden vulnerabilities that attackers exploit to bypass segmentation controls and move laterally within the network.

Balancing security and operational efficiency is another key challenge in network segmentation. While strict segmentation policies enhance security by limiting access between different parts of the network, they can also create operational bottlenecks if not designed properly.

Excessive segmentation can result in increased latency, broken application dependencies, and workflow disruptions that hinder productivity. IT teams often face resistance from business units that rely on seamless communication between systems. Striking the right balance requires continuous monitoring of network traffic, collaboration between security and operations teams, and regular policy reviews to ensure that segmentation does not impede critical business functions.

The evolving nature of IT environments makes it difficult to maintain effective segmentation over time. Modern enterprises frequently undergo infrastructure changes, such as cloud migrations, software updates, and network expansions. As new applications and services are introduced, segmentation policies must be updated accordingly to reflect changes in network architecture. Organizations that fail to regularly audit and update their segmentation policies risk creating outdated rules that no longer align with their security posture. Legacy systems further complicate the process, as many older devices and applications were not designed with segmentation in mind, making integration with modern segmentation frameworks challenging.

Cloud and hybrid environments introduce additional segmentation complexities. Traditional segmentation models were designed for on-premises networks with clearly defined perimeters, but cloud computing has blurred these boundaries. Organizations using multi-cloud and hybrid cloud architectures must implement segmentation policies that span across different cloud providers while ensuring seamless integration with on-premises infrastructure. Each cloud provider has its own set of security tools and network configurations, making it challenging to enforce consistent segmentation policies. Managing segmentation across multiple environments requires the use of software-defined networking (SDN) and microsegmentation solutions that provide centralized policy control and automation.

Lack of visibility into network traffic and segmentation effectiveness is another common challenge. Organizations need a clear understanding of how devices, users, and applications communicate within the network to create effective segmentation policies. Without proper visibility, IT teams may struggle to identify unauthorized access attempts, segmentation violations, or misconfigured rules. Security

Information and Event Management (SIEM) systems, network monitoring tools, and threat intelligence platforms can help improve visibility, but they require continuous tuning to provide meaningful insights. Without real-time monitoring, organizations may not detect segmentation weaknesses until a security incident occurs.

User and device management presents an ongoing challenge in network segmentation. As workforces become more mobile and remote work becomes the norm, users connect to corporate networks from a variety of devices, locations, and networks. Traditional segmentation approaches struggle to enforce consistent security policies across an increasingly dynamic workforce. Identity-based segmentation and Zero Trust security models offer solutions by enforcing access controls based on user identity, device posture, and contextual factors. However, implementing identity-based segmentation requires integration with identity and access management (IAM) systems and continuous authentication mechanisms, which can be complex to manage.

Compliance and regulatory requirements add another layer of complexity to segmentation. Many industries are required to implement strict access controls to protect sensitive data, such as financial records, healthcare information, and payment card data. While segmentation helps organizations meet these compliance requirements, failing to properly implement segmentation policies can result in non-compliance. Auditing and maintaining compliance records for segmented networks can be a time-consuming process, requiring extensive documentation of access controls, segmentation policies, and security monitoring efforts. Organizations must ensure that their segmentation strategies align with regulatory frameworks such as GDPR, PCI DSS, HIPAA, and NIST guidelines.

Security threats are constantly evolving, requiring organizations to adapt their segmentation strategies accordingly. Attackers continue to develop new methods for bypassing segmentation controls, exploiting misconfigurations, and leveraging insider threats to gain access to sensitive systems. Ransomware attacks, for example, often rely on lateral movement to spread within a network, making segmentation a critical defense mechanism. Organizations must conduct regular security assessments, penetration testing, and red team exercises to validate the effectiveness of their segmentation policies. Without proactive security testing, organizations may not realize that their segmentation controls are inadequate until a breach occurs.

The challenge of automation and orchestration in segmentation remains a barrier for many organizations. Traditional segmentation approaches require extensive manual configuration, which is difficult to scale in complex environments. Modern segmentation solutions leverage automation and orchestration to dynamically enforce policies based on real-time network activity. However, integrating automation into existing network infrastructure requires careful planning and investment in security tools that support policy-driven segmentation. Organizations that fail to embrace automation may struggle to keep up with the rapid pace of network changes, leading to security gaps and increased administrative burden.

Despite these challenges, network segmentation remains one of the most effective security strategies for protecting sensitive data, preventing unauthorized access, and enhancing overall cybersecurity. Organizations that take a proactive approach to addressing segmentation challenges can create a more secure, efficient, and resilient network environment. By leveraging automation, improving visibility, enforcing identity-based policies, and continuously updating segmentation strategies, businesses can overcome the complexities of segmentation and strengthen their defenses against evolving cyber threats.

Zero Trust and Microsegmentation

Zero Trust and microsegmentation are two critical security concepts that work together to create a robust defense against modern cyber threats. As organizations move away from traditional perimeter-based security models, the need for granular access controls and dynamic security policies has become increasingly important. Zero Trust operates on the fundamental principle that no entity—whether inside or outside the network—should be inherently trusted. Instead, every request for access must be authenticated, authorized, and continuously verified. Microsegmentation complements this approach by enforcing strict access controls at the workload level, ensuring that even within a network, communication is limited to only what is necessary.

Traditional security models relied on the assumption that internal networks were inherently safe, focusing defenses primarily on external threats. Firewalls, perimeter defenses, and intrusion detection systems were designed to block malicious traffic from the outside while allowing trusted internal traffic to flow freely. However, this approach has become obsolete due to the increasing sophistication of cyber threats, the rise of cloud computing, remote work, and the expansion of attack surfaces. Once attackers bypass a perimeter defense, they often have unrestricted access to internal systems, allowing them to move laterally across the network with minimal resistance. Zero Trust and microsegmentation address these shortcomings by eliminating implicit trust and enforcing least-privilege access policies.

Zero Trust is based on several core principles that redefine how organizations secure their networks. One of the primary tenets is the principle of least privilege, which ensures that users, devices, and applications are granted only the minimal level of access required to perform their functions. This approach significantly reduces the risk of unauthorized access and limits the potential damage of a security breach. Another key aspect of Zero Trust is continuous verification, which requires ongoing authentication and authorization of all entities attempting to access network resources. Instead of relying on a one-time authentication process, Zero Trust mandates that access be continuously evaluated based on real-time security assessments, user behavior, and contextual factors such as device health, geolocation, and network conditions.

Microsegmentation is a crucial component of Zero Trust because it allows organizations to enforce granular security controls across their entire infrastructure. Unlike traditional network segmentation, which typically operates at the VLAN or subnet level, microsegmentation creates security boundaries at the workload, application, or even process level. This ensures that even within a trusted network segment, individual workloads are isolated from each other unless explicitly permitted to communicate. By applying Zero Trust principles at a micro level, organizations can minimize the risk of lateral movement and contain threats before they spread across the network.

One of the key benefits of microsegmentation within a Zero Trust framework is its ability to prevent ransomware and other advanced threats from propagating. Ransomware attacks often rely on lateral movement to spread from an initially compromised device to other critical systems within the network. In a flat network, once an attacker gains access, they can easily move between systems, escalate privileges, and encrypt or exfiltrate data. Microsegmentation blocks this movement by restricting communication between workloads to only what is explicitly required. Even if a device is compromised, the attack is contained within a small, isolated environment, significantly limiting the impact of the breach.

Cloud environments present unique challenges that make Zero Trust and microsegmentation even more essential. Traditional network security measures were designed for static, on-premises infrastructures with well-defined perimeters. However, modern organizations operate in hybrid and multi-cloud environments where workloads are constantly shifting between on-premises data centers, public clouds, and edge computing environments. In such dynamic ecosystems, relying on perimeter-based security models is ineffective, as there is no clear boundary to defend. Zero Trust and microsegmentation provide a scalable security solution that adapts to cloud-native architectures, allowing organizations to enforce security policies based on identity, context, and workload attributes rather than static network boundaries.

Implementing microsegmentation within a Zero Trust architecture requires a deep understanding of network traffic patterns and application dependencies. Organizations must first conduct a thorough mapping of their network to identify how workloads interact and what communication paths are necessary for business operations. This visibility is crucial for defining effective microsegmentation policies that strike the right balance between security and functionality. Overly restrictive policies can disrupt normal operations, while overly permissive policies can leave security gaps that attackers could exploit. Security teams must work closely with application owners, IT administrators, and business leaders to design policies that enforce Zero Trust principles without hindering productivity.

Automation and artificial intelligence play a significant role in the successful deployment of Zero Trust and microsegmentation. Given the complexity of modern IT environments, manually managing security policies for thousands of workloads is impractical. Advanced security solutions leverage AI-driven analytics to analyze network traffic, detect anomalies, and dynamically adjust microsegmentation policies based on real-time threats. Machine learning models can identify normal communication patterns and automatically generate segmentation rules that minimize security risks while maintaining operational efficiency. By integrating AI and automation into Zero Trust and microsegmentation strategies, organizations can reduce administrative overhead, improve response times, and enhance their overall security posture.

Identity-based security is another crucial aspect of Zero Trust that aligns with microsegmentation. Instead of granting access based solely on IP addresses or network locations, Zero Trust enforces policies based on user identities, device health, and contextual risk factors. This approach ensures that access decisions are not dependent on static network configurations but rather on continuously updated risk assessments. By integrating identity and access management (IAM) solutions with microsegmentation policies, organizations can ensure that users and applications are only allowed to interact with the resources necessary for their specific roles.

The integration of Zero Trust and microsegmentation also enhances compliance with regulatory requirements. Many industries, including healthcare, finance, and government sectors, must adhere to strict data protection regulations such as HIPAA, PCI DSS, and GDPR. These regulations mandate strict access controls, data segmentation, and continuous monitoring to protect sensitive information. By implementing a Zero Trust model with microsegmentation, organizations can enforce compliance controls at a granular level, ensuring that sensitive data remains isolated, access is strictly controlled, and security policies are continuously enforced and audited.

Organizations that successfully implement Zero Trust and microsegmentation gain a significant security advantage in protecting against cyber threats, reducing attack surfaces, and ensuring business continuity. As cyber adversaries continue to evolve their tactics, relying on traditional perimeter-based defenses is no longer sufficient. A Zero Trust architecture, reinforced by microsegmentation, provides a proactive security approach that dynamically adapts to modern IT environments, minimizing risks and enabling organizations to maintain control over their digital assets. By adopting this security model, businesses can build a resilient infrastructure that prioritizes security, minimizes exposure to cyber threats, and ensures the integrity of their critical systems and data.

Network Segmentation Strategies

Network segmentation is a crucial security and performance optimization technique that involves dividing a network into smaller, isolated segments to control traffic flow and restrict access between different parts of the network. Effective segmentation helps prevent cyber threats from spreading, enhances regulatory compliance, and improves overall network efficiency. However, implementing a segmentation strategy requires careful planning, a deep understanding of network traffic, and a balance between security and operational requirements. Organizations must adopt the right segmentation strategies based on their infrastructure, business needs, and security posture to ensure both protection and functionality.

One of the foundational approaches to network segmentation is physical segmentation, which involves separating network environments using dedicated hardware such as routers, switches, and firewalls. This method physically isolates different segments of the network, ensuring that devices in one segment cannot communicate directly with devices in another segment unless explicitly allowed through controlled pathways. Physical segmentation is commonly used in highly secure environments such as data centers, government facilities, and industrial control systems, where strict isolation is required to prevent unauthorized access. However, this approach can be expensive and difficult to scale, as it requires additional infrastructure for each new segment.

Logical segmentation offers a more flexible alternative by using software-based methods to divide the network. This approach does not require dedicated physical infrastructure but instead relies on technologies such as VLANs, access control lists (ACLs), and firewalls to create isolated segments within a shared network. VLAN segmentation allows administrators to group devices logically, regardless of their physical location, ensuring that different departments, applications, or user groups have separate network environments. ACLs define rules that govern which traffic is allowed between segments, preventing unauthorized access while allowing necessary communication. While logical segmentation is more scalable than physical segmentation, misconfigurations can create vulnerabilities if not properly managed.

Role-based segmentation is another widely used strategy that enforces access controls based on user roles, device types, or application functions. In this model, network policies are defined based on business requirements, ensuring that employees, contractors, guests, and critical systems are kept separate from one another. For example, an organization may segment its network so that finance department employees can only access financial applications, while developers have access to software repositories but not sensitive customer data. This type of segmentation is particularly effective in large enterprises where multiple user groups require access to different resources.

Application-aware segmentation enhances security by defining network policies based on application behaviors rather than traditional IP-based rules. Many modern cyber threats exploit vulnerabilities in applications, making it essential to enforce segmentation based on how applications interact with each other and with the network. In this strategy, security policies are dynamically applied to control which applications can communicate and under what conditions. Application-layer firewalls, deep packet inspection (DPI), and next-generation security solutions enable organizations to enforce granular controls, ensuring that only authorized applications are allowed to exchange data. This approach is especially beneficial in cloud environments where applications are distributed across different infrastructure components.

Microsegmentation is an advanced network segmentation strategy that provides workload-level security by isolating applications, virtual machines, and services from each other, even within the same network segment. Unlike traditional segmentation methods, which rely on subnets and VLANs, microsegmentation enforces policies at a much finer level, ensuring that only explicitly authorized connections are permitted. This strategy is particularly useful in cloud environments, hybrid infrastructures, and highly dynamic IT ecosystems where traditional segmentation is insufficient. Microsegmentation leverages identity-based controls, machine learning, and software-defined networking (SDN) to enforce security policies dynamically, reducing the risk of lateral movement in the event of a breach.

Environment-based segmentation is commonly used to separate development, testing, and production environments within an organization's IT infrastructure. Development and testing environments often involve frequent changes, untested code, and experimental configurations that could introduce security risks if not properly isolated. By segmenting these environments, organizations can prevent unauthorized access to production systems and ensure that any vulnerabilities in non-production environments do not affect mission-critical applications. This approach is essential for software development teams that require flexibility while maintaining a secure and controlled production environment.

Network segmentation strategies must also consider the integration of cloud and hybrid environments. As businesses migrate workloads to cloud platforms, traditional segmentation methods may not be sufficient to provide consistent security across multiple infrastructures. Cloud-native segmentation strategies leverage cloud security groups, network security policies, and software-defined perimeters to enforce access controls dynamically. Organizations using hybrid cloud architectures must implement segmentation strategies that span across on-premises and cloud environments while maintaining consistent security policies. The use of cloud access security brokers (CASBs) and cloud-native security tools allows organizations to extend segmentation controls across distributed environments without compromising security.

Regulatory compliance often drives the need for specific segmentation strategies, particularly in industries that handle sensitive data. Financial institutions, healthcare organizations, and government agencies are required to adhere to strict compliance standards such as PCI DSS, HIPAA, and GDPR, which mandate strict access controls to protect sensitive information. Regulatory segmentation strategies ensure that data is stored, transmitted, and accessed according to compliance requirements, preventing unauthorized access and reducing the risk of data breaches. Organizations must implement auditing and monitoring tools to verify that segmentation policies align with regulatory frameworks and that access control logs are regularly reviewed.

Implementing an effective segmentation strategy requires continuous monitoring and policy enforcement to adapt to changing network conditions. Many organizations struggle with maintaining segmentation over time due to evolving infrastructure, application dependencies, and shifting security threats. Automated segmentation solutions help address this challenge by continuously analyzing network traffic, identifying anomalies, and dynamically adjusting segmentation rules based on real-time security intelligence. Artificial intelligence (AI) and machine learning (ML) technologies enhance segmentation by detecting suspicious behavior and preventing unauthorized access without manual intervention. Organizations that leverage automation can reduce the complexity of segmentation management while ensuring that security policies remain up to date.

Network segmentation strategies must also consider the role of Zero Trust security models in modern environments. Zero Trust operates on the principle that no entity—whether inside or outside the network—should be automatically trusted. Instead, access decisions are based on identity, device compliance, and contextual risk factors. When combined with segmentation, Zero Trust ensures that access is strictly controlled at every level, preventing unauthorized movement within the network. Organizations adopting Zero Trust segmentation enforce least-privilege access policies, requiring continuous authentication and authorization for all network interactions. This model significantly reduces the risk of data breaches by eliminating excessive trust relationships between network components.

Organizations that invest in well-defined segmentation strategies gain several advantages, including improved security, reduced risk exposure, enhanced network performance, and regulatory compliance. Whether using traditional VLANs, microsegmentation, cloud-native security controls, or identity-based segmentation, businesses must carefully plan their segmentation approach to align with their security objectives and operational requirements. As cyber threats continue to evolve, the need for effective segmentation strategies becomes even more critical in protecting sensitive assets, preventing unauthorized access, and ensuring the integrity of enterprise networks. By adopting a proactive approach to segmentation, organizations can create a resilient security framework that minimizes risks while supporting business agility and growth.

VLANs and Their Role in Segmentation

Virtual Local Area Networks, or VLANs, play a crucial role in network segmentation by enabling logical separation of devices within a physical network infrastructure. VLANs allow network administrators to group devices based on function, department, or security requirements, rather than physical location. This logical segmentation improves security, optimizes network performance, and enhances manageability by reducing unnecessary traffic between different network segments. As organizations expand their networks and adopt complex IT infrastructures, VLANs become an essential tool for enforcing access controls and maintaining efficient data flow.

Traditional network architectures often rely on flat, unsegmented networks where all devices communicate freely. This approach, while simple, introduces significant security risks and performance bottlenecks. A flat network means that all devices, regardless of their role, share the same broadcast domain, leading to excessive traffic congestion and increased exposure to cyber threats. VLANs address these challenges by logically segmenting devices into separate network domains, each with its own broadcast boundaries. This isolation ensures that network traffic is confined within specific VLANs, reducing congestion and limiting the potential spread of security threats.

Security is one of the primary reasons organizations implement VLANs for segmentation. In an unsegmented network, a compromised device can communicate with any other device on the network, allowing attackers to move laterally and access sensitive systems. By using VLANs, organizations can create isolated segments that prevent unauthorized communication between devices. For example, a company can assign employees, guests, and IoT devices to separate VLANs, ensuring that guest users cannot access internal systems and IoT devices remain isolated from corporate applications. This approach significantly reduces the attack surface and mitigates the risk of cyber intrusions.

VLANs also play a key role in enforcing access control policies. Network administrators can define rules that dictate which VLANs can communicate with each other using access control lists (ACLs) and firewalls. These policies ensure that only authorized traffic flows between VLANs, preventing unauthorized access to sensitive data. For example, an organization may implement ACLs that allow HR systems to communicate with payroll servers while blocking access from other VLANs. This level of control enhances security by restricting access to sensitive information based on predefined policies.

Performance optimization is another major benefit of VLANs in network segmentation. In large networks, excessive broadcast traffic can degrade performance, leading to increased latency and reduced bandwidth availability. VLANs alleviate this issue by confining broadcast traffic to specific segments, preventing unnecessary data transmission across the entire network. This improves efficiency by ensuring that only relevant devices receive broadcast messages, reducing network congestion and enhancing overall performance. By segmenting traffic based on usage patterns, organizations can allocate bandwidth more effectively, ensuring that critical applications receive the necessary resources.

Scalability is an important consideration for growing organizations, and VLANs provide a flexible solution for managing network expansion. As new departments, remote offices, or cloud services are added, VLANs can be configured to accommodate these changes without requiring significant infrastructure modifications. Unlike physical segmentation, which requires additional hardware and cabling, VLANs allow administrators to create new segments dynamically using software-based configurations. This flexibility enables organizations to adapt to changing business needs while maintaining a structured and secure network architecture.

VLAN trunking is an advanced feature that allows multiple VLANs to share a single network link while maintaining logical separation. Using protocols such as IEEE 802.1Q, VLAN trunks tag Ethernet frames with VLAN identifiers, enabling traffic from different VLANs to be transmitted over the same physical connection. This approach optimizes network resources by reducing the need for multiple dedicated links while preserving segmentation. VLAN trunking is commonly used in data centers, enterprise networks, and multi-tenant environments where multiple VLANs must communicate across a shared infrastructure.

Despite their benefits, VLANs are not immune to security risks. VLAN hopping is a well-known attack technique that exploits misconfigurations to bypass segmentation controls and gain unauthorized access to other VLANs. Attackers can use methods such as double-tagging and switch spoofing to manipulate VLAN traffic and escalate privileges within a network. To mitigate VLAN hopping risks, organizations must implement strict security measures, including disabling unused ports, enabling port security, and applying proper VLAN tagging configurations. Regular security audits and network monitoring help detect and prevent potential vulnerabilities before they can be exploited.

Integration with other segmentation technologies enhances the effectiveness of VLANs in securing modern networks. While VLANs provide logical isolation, additional security layers such as microsegmentation, firewalls, and Zero Trust policies further restrict access based on identity, behavior, and contextual factors. Combining VLANs with microsegmentation allows organizations to enforce granular security policies at the workload level, ensuring that even within a VLAN, individual devices or applications remain isolated unless explicitly permitted to communicate. This hybrid approach strengthens security while maintaining the scalability and efficiency of VLAN-based segmentation.

Cloud adoption and hybrid IT environments present new challenges for VLAN-based segmentation. Traditional VLANs were designed for on-premises networks with well-defined physical boundaries, but cloud environments introduce dynamic workloads that require adaptive segmentation strategies. Organizations must extend VLANs across hybrid cloud architectures using virtualized networking solutions such as Virtual Extensible LAN (VXLAN) and software-defined networking (SDN). These technologies enable seamless VLAN segmentation across on-premises and cloud environments, ensuring consistent security policies regardless of where workloads reside.

The role of VLANs in network segmentation extends beyond security and performance to compliance and regulatory requirements. Many industries are subject to strict data protection regulations that mandate controlled access to sensitive information. VLANs help organizations meet compliance requirements by isolating data based on regulatory classifications. For example, a financial institution can use VLANs to separate customer transaction data from general network traffic, ensuring compliance with PCI DSS standards. Similarly, healthcare organizations can use VLAN segmentation to protect electronic health records in accordance with HIPAA regulations.

Proper VLAN management is essential to maintaining an effective segmentation strategy. Organizations must establish clear VLAN naming conventions, document segmentation policies, and regularly audit network configurations to ensure compliance with security best practices. Misconfigured VLANs can lead to unintended access permissions, network instability, and security vulnerabilities. Network administrators should implement automated monitoring tools to track VLAN traffic, detect anomalies, and enforce security policies in real time. Continuous assessment and refinement of VLAN configurations ensure that segmentation remains aligned with organizational security goals.

As cyber threats become more sophisticated and network environments grow increasingly complex, VLANs continue to be a foundational tool for network segmentation. While VLANs alone cannot provide complete security, they serve as a critical first layer of defense in a multi-layered security approach. By integrating VLAN segmentation with advanced security frameworks, organizations can create a resilient network architecture that minimizes risks, optimizes performance, and supports the evolving demands of modern IT infrastructures. A well-designed VLAN strategy enhances both security and efficiency, ensuring that networks remain protected while enabling seamless communication between authorized users and applications.

Implementing Firewall-Based Segmentation

Firewall-based segmentation is a fundamental strategy for securing modern networks by controlling and restricting traffic flow between different segments. Firewalls serve as gatekeepers, enforcing security policies that determine which devices, applications, and users can communicate across network boundaries. By implementing firewall-based segmentation, organizations can strengthen security, reduce attack surfaces, and prevent unauthorized lateral movement. A well-designed firewall segmentation strategy ensures that sensitive data and critical infrastructure remain isolated while allowing legitimate communication to occur seamlessly.

Traditional network security models relied on perimeter firewalls to protect against external threats. These firewalls were positioned at the edge of the network, filtering incoming and outgoing traffic based on predefined rules. While perimeter defenses remain important, they are no longer sufficient in today's dynamic IT environments. Modern networks span on-premises data centers, cloud infrastructures, remote offices, and mobile devices, requiring more granular segmentation controls. Firewall-based segmentation extends beyond perimeter security by enforcing policies at various points within the network, ensuring that internal threats are contained and security is maintained at every level.

The first step in implementing firewall-based segmentation is defining security zones. Security zones are logical network segments that group devices, users, and applications based on function, sensitivity, or risk level. For example, an organization may create separate security zones for internal workstations, cloud applications, IoT devices, and third-party vendors. Each zone is protected by a firewall, which enforces rules that control how traffic flows between segments. By defining clear security zones, organizations can minimize the risk of unauthorized access and prevent security breaches from spreading across the network.

Firewalls enforce segmentation policies using access control rules that specify which traffic is allowed or denied between security zones. These rules are based on factors such as source and destination IP addresses, ports, protocols, and application types. Administrators must carefully design firewall rules to ensure that only necessary traffic is permitted while blocking unauthorized connections. A common best practice is to follow the principle of least privilege, allowing only the minimum level of access required for business operations. Overly permissive firewall rules can expose networks to cyber threats, while overly restrictive rules may disrupt legitimate communication. Striking the right balance is essential for maintaining both security and usability.

Next-generation firewalls (NGFWs) enhance firewall-based segmentation by providing advanced security capabilities beyond traditional packet filtering. NGFWs incorporate deep packet inspection (DPI), intrusion prevention systems (IPS), application-layer filtering, and user-based access controls. These features enable organizations to create more precise segmentation policies that go beyond basic network parameters. For example, rather than simply allowing or blocking traffic based on IP addresses, NGFWs can enforce policies based on application behavior, user identity, or real-time threat intelligence. This level of granularity ensures that segmentation rules adapt to evolving security threats and business requirements.

One of the key benefits of firewall-based segmentation is the ability to prevent lateral movement within a network. In a flat, unsegmented network, once an attacker gains access to a single compromised device, they can move laterally to other systems with little resistance. Firewalls restrict this movement by enforcing strict controls on internal traffic, ensuring that devices and applications can only communicate if explicitly permitted. For example, an organization can configure firewall rules to prevent workstations from directly communicating with servers, forcing all requests to pass through secure application gateways. This approach limits an attacker's ability to escalate privileges or access sensitive data.

Firewall segmentation is particularly effective in protecting critical infrastructure, such as data centers, cloud environments, and industrial control systems. Data centers house sensitive applications and databases that require strict access controls to prevent data breaches. By segmenting data center resources with firewalls, organizations can enforce security policies that restrict access to only authorized users and applications. In cloud environments, firewall-based segmentation helps ensure that virtual machines, containers, and cloud services remain isolated from each other, reducing the risk of data leakage and unauthorized access. Industrial control systems, which operate critical infrastructure such as power grids and manufacturing plants, benefit from segmentation by preventing cyber threats from disrupting operations.

The rise of Zero Trust security models has further reinforced the importance of firewall-based segmentation. Zero Trust operates on the principle that no device, user, or application should be trusted by default, requiring continuous verification before granting access. Firewall-based segmentation aligns with Zero Trust by enforcing strict access controls between network segments and dynamically adjusting policies based on real-time security assessments. Organizations implementing Zero Trust can leverage firewalls to enforce identity-based access controls, ensuring that only authenticated and authorized entities can communicate across network boundaries.

One of the challenges in implementing firewall-based segmentation is managing rule complexity. Large organizations may have thousands of firewall rules governing traffic between different segments, making it difficult to ensure consistency and compliance. Poorly managed firewall policies can lead to security gaps, redundant rules, and misconfigurations that weaken segmentation effectiveness. To address this challenge, organizations should implement centralized firewall management solutions that provide visibility into rule configurations, automate policy enforcement, and detect anomalies. Regular audits and rule reviews help ensure that firewall policies remain aligned with security best practices and business objectives.

Automating firewall segmentation policies can significantly improve security and operational efficiency. Traditional firewall management requires manual configuration of rules, which is time-consuming and prone to human error. Modern security solutions integrate with automation platforms to dynamically enforce segmentation policies based on real-time network activity and threat intelligence. For example, if a security monitoring system detects suspicious behavior in a specific network segment, automated firewall policies can immediately isolate the affected segment, preventing the potential spread of an attack. Automation also enables organizations to scale their segmentation strategies without increasing administrative overhead.

Firewall-based segmentation also plays a critical role in regulatory compliance. Many industry regulations require organizations to implement strict access controls to protect sensitive data and ensure compliance with security standards. The Payment Card Industry Data Security Standard (PCI DSS) mandates that organizations handling credit card transactions segment cardholder data environments from other network components. The Health Insurance Portability and Accountability Act (HIPAA) requires healthcare organizations to enforce strict security controls to protect patient information. Firewall segmentation helps organizations meet these compliance requirements by isolating sensitive data, enforcing access policies, and generating audit logs for security monitoring.

As cyber threats continue to evolve, firewall-based segmentation remains a foundational security measure for protecting enterprise networks. Organizations must continuously refine their segmentation strategies to address emerging risks, optimize performance, and adapt to new business needs. By integrating next-generation firewall capabilities, leveraging automation, and aligning segmentation with Zero Trust principles, businesses can enhance their security posture while maintaining operational efficiency. Firewall-based segmentation is a proactive approach to cybersecurity, providing organizations with the necessary controls to safeguard critical assets, prevent lateral movement, and ensure secure communication across complex IT environments.

Software-Defined Networking (SDN) and Segmentation

Software-Defined Networking (SDN) has revolutionized the way organizations design, manage, and secure their networks. By decoupling the control plane from the data plane, SDN allows centralized network control through software rather than relying on traditional hardware configurations. This shift provides greater flexibility, automation, and programmability, making SDN a powerful tool for implementing network segmentation. In modern IT environments, where networks span across data centers, cloud infrastructures, and edge devices, SDN enhances segmentation by enabling dynamic, policy-driven traffic control that adapts to changing network conditions and security requirements.

Traditional network segmentation relied heavily on physical infrastructure, VLANs, and manually configured access control lists (ACLs). These methods, while effective in static environments, struggled to keep up with the growing complexity of distributed networks, mobile workforces, and cloud computing. Changes to network segmentation required manual intervention, increasing the risk of misconfigurations and security gaps. SDN addresses these limitations by allowing network administrators to define segmentation policies programmatically, automating policy enforcement across multiple network segments. This level of automation ensures that segmentation remains consistent and up to date, reducing the operational burden of maintaining security policies across large-scale networks.

One of the primary benefits of SDN-based segmentation is its ability to provide fine-grained control over traffic flows. Unlike traditional segmentation methods that operate at the subnet or VLAN level, SDN enables microsegmentation by enforcing security policies at the workload, application, or user level. This ensures that only authorized entities can communicate with each other, significantly reducing the risk of lateral movement within the network. By leveraging SDN controllers, organizations can create dynamic segmentation rules that automatically adjust based on real-time network activity, security threats, or workload requirements. This capability is particularly beneficial in environments where workloads are frequently moved between on-premises data centers and cloud platforms.

SDN simplifies network segmentation by centralizing policy management. In traditional networks, segmentation rules were distributed across multiple network devices, including routers, switches, and firewalls. Each device required individual configuration, making it difficult to maintain consistency and troubleshoot segmentation policies. SDN centralizes these controls within an SDN controller, which acts as the brain of the network, defining segmentation policies that are then enforced across all connected devices. This centralized approach eliminates inconsistencies, reduces administrative overhead, and allows for faster deployment of security policies. Organizations can define segmentation rules once and have them automatically applied across the entire network, ensuring uniform security enforcement.

Security automation is another key advantage of using SDN for segmentation. SDN integrates with security monitoring tools, threat intelligence platforms, and intrusion detection systems to dynamically enforce security policies in response to detected threats. If a security monitoring system identifies malicious activity in a particular segment, SDN can instantly isolate the affected segment by updating flow rules in the SDN controller. This rapid response capability minimizes the impact of cyberattacks by containing threats before they spread across the network. Additionally, SDN's programmability allows organizations to implement Zero Trust principles, enforcing strict access controls based on user identity, device health, and contextual risk factors.

Cloud environments benefit significantly from SDN-based segmentation due to their dynamic and elastic nature. Traditional segmentation approaches were designed for static networks with well-defined perimeters, but cloud computing introduces fluid workloads that move between different environments. SDN provides the agility needed to enforce segmentation policies in multi-cloud and hybrid cloud architectures, ensuring that security policies remain consistent regardless of where workloads reside. Organizations using SDN can define segmentation policies that extend across cloud providers, enabling secure communication between on-premises data centers, private clouds, and public cloud platforms. This cross-environment segmentation capability is essential for organizations adopting cloud-first strategies.

The role of SDN in segmentation extends beyond security to network performance optimization. In traditional networks, segmentation policies were often implemented using static firewall rules or VLAN configurations that could lead to inefficient traffic routing. SDN enables intelligent traffic engineering by dynamically adjusting segmentation policies based on network conditions. By analyzing real-time traffic patterns, SDN can prioritize critical application traffic, reduce congestion, and optimize bandwidth allocation across different segments. This level of control ensures that segmentation does not negatively impact performance while maintaining strong security boundaries.

Network Function Virtualization (NFV) enhances SDN-based segmentation by virtualizing network services such as firewalls, load balancers, and intrusion prevention systems. In traditional networks, these security functions were deployed as physical appliances, requiring dedicated hardware for each segment. With NFV, security services can be instantiated as virtualized functions, enabling flexible and scalable segmentation without additional hardware costs. SDN orchestrates these virtualized security functions, ensuring that segmentation policies are enforced dynamically across distributed environments. The combination of SDN and NFV allows organizations to build agile, software-defined security architectures that adapt to evolving threats and business requirements.

One of the challenges in implementing SDN-based segmentation is ensuring interoperability with existing network infrastructure. Many organizations operate hybrid environments that include legacy hardware, traditional networking protocols, and software-defined components. Migrating to an SDN-based segmentation model requires careful planning to ensure compatibility between legacy systems and SDN controllers. Organizations must assess their existing network architecture, evaluate SDN solutions that support hybrid deployments, and gradually transition to software-defined segmentation without disrupting critical business operations. Vendor support, open standards, and API integrations play a crucial role in facilitating this transition.

Visibility and monitoring are essential for maintaining effective SDN-based segmentation. Traditional network monitoring tools were designed to analyze traffic flows based on static configurations, but SDN introduces dynamic policy enforcement that requires continuous visibility into network behavior. Organizations must deploy SDN-compatible monitoring solutions that provide real-time insights into segmentation policies, traffic patterns, and security events. These tools enable security teams to detect anomalies, identify misconfigurations, and ensure that segmentation policies align with business objectives. By leveraging SDN analytics and telemetry data, organizations can fine-tune their segmentation strategies for maximum security and efficiency.

Regulatory compliance is another factor driving the adoption of SDN-based segmentation. Many industries require strict access controls, data isolation, and security auditing to meet regulatory requirements such as GDPR, HIPAA, and PCI DSS. SDN facilitates compliance by automating segmentation policies, logging security events, and enforcing least-privilege access models. Organizations can define compliance-driven segmentation rules that automatically adjust to regulatory changes, reducing the risk of non-compliance. By integrating SDN with compliance monitoring tools, businesses can generate audit-ready reports that demonstrate adherence to security best practices and regulatory mandates.

As cyber threats become more sophisticated and networks continue to expand, SDN-based segmentation provides a scalable, automated, and security-centric approach to protecting digital assets. By decoupling segmentation policies from traditional hardware limitations, SDN enables organizations to enforce granular security controls, optimize network performance, and maintain agility in dynamic IT environments. The integration of SDN with security automation, cloud-native architectures, and Zero Trust frameworks ensures that segmentation remains a proactive defense mechanism rather than a static network constraint. Organizations that embrace SDN-based segmentation gain the ability to secure their networks more effectively while maintaining the flexibility needed to support modern business operations.

Network Access Control (NAC) and Segmentation

Network Access Control (NAC) plays a crucial role in enforcing security policies and managing network segmentation by controlling which devices and users can access specific network segments. As cyber threats continue to evolve, organizations must implement strict access controls to prevent unauthorized access and protect sensitive assets. NAC provides a centralized framework for verifying user identities, assessing device compliance, and enforcing segmentation policies dynamically. By integrating NAC with network segmentation strategies, organizations can ensure that only authorized entities gain access to specific areas of the network while maintaining security, compliance, and operational efficiency.

Traditional network environments relied on basic access control mechanisms, such as usernames and passwords, to regulate network access. However, this approach has proven insufficient in today's complex IT environments, where users connect from various locations, using multiple devices, and accessing both on-premises and cloud-based resources. The rapid adoption of remote work, bring-your-own-device (BYOD) policies, and Internet of Things (IoT) deployments has further expanded the attack surface, making traditional access control inadequate. NAC addresses these challenges by enforcing strict authentication and authorization policies before allowing devices or users to connect to the network.

One of the fundamental functions of NAC in segmentation is authentication and identity verification. NAC solutions use authentication mechanisms such as 802.1X, RADIUS, and multi-factor authentication (MFA) to verify users and devices before granting access to network resources. Organizations can configure NAC policies to authenticate users based on credentials, certificates, or biometric authentication, ensuring that only legitimate users are granted network access. This authentication process prevents unauthorized users from connecting to the network and accessing sensitive data or systems.

Device compliance checks are another critical component of NAC in segmentation. Organizations must ensure that only secure and compliant devices can access the network, minimizing the risk of malware infections, data breaches, and unauthorized access attempts. NAC solutions assess device health by checking for up-to-date antivirus software, security patches, firewall configurations, and endpoint protection policies. If a device fails to meet security requirements, NAC can quarantine the device, redirect it to a remediation network, or deny access entirely. This proactive approach prevents compromised or non-compliant devices from introducing security risks into the segmented network.

NAC enables dynamic segmentation by assigning network access policies based on user roles, device types, and contextual factors. Unlike traditional segmentation methods that rely on static VLANs or subnet-based access controls, NAC dynamically assigns users and devices to appropriate network segments based on predefined security policies. For example, an employee accessing the network from a corporate laptop may be assigned to a trusted internal segment, while a contractor using a personal device may be restricted to a limited-access guest segment. This level of segmentation ensures that users only have access to the resources necessary for their specific roles, reducing the risk of unauthorized lateral movement within the network.

Zero Trust security models align closely with NAC and network segmentation by enforcing the principle of least privilege. In a Zero Trust environment, no user or device is automatically trusted, and access decisions are continuously verified based on real-time security assessments. NAC plays a key role in enforcing Zero Trust segmentation by verifying identity, assessing risk levels, and enforcing adaptive access controls. If a user attempts to access a restricted segment or if NAC detects anomalous behavior, access can be immediately revoked, preventing potential security breaches. This dynamic and continuous verification process strengthens network segmentation by ensuring that access is always granted based on contextual risk factors rather than static trust models.

Microsegmentation further enhances NAC-based segmentation by applying granular access controls at the workload and application level. While NAC enforces access control at the network level, microsegmentation ensures that even within an authorized segment, communication is restricted based on identity, application behavior, and security policies. For example, an authenticated user may be granted access to a corporate network segment but restricted from communicating with critical infrastructure or high-value applications. The combination of NAC and microsegmentation creates a multi-layered security approach that minimizes attack surfaces and prevents unauthorized movement across network segments.

IoT security is a growing concern that NAC helps address within segmented networks. IoT devices, such as smart cameras, industrial sensors, and medical equipment, often have limited security capabilities and cannot be directly secured using traditional endpoint protection tools. NAC enables organizations to segment IoT devices from core business networks, ensuring that these potentially vulnerable devices cannot be used as entry points for cyberattacks. By isolating IoT traffic into dedicated network segments and enforcing strict access controls, NAC prevents compromised IoT devices from being exploited to gain access to critical systems or data.

Cloud environments present unique challenges for NAC-based segmentation, as traditional network boundaries no longer apply in multi-cloud and hybrid infrastructures. Organizations must enforce consistent access control policies across on-premises data centers, public cloud platforms, and remote access networks. NAC solutions that integrate with cloud identity providers and security frameworks allow organizations to extend segmentation policies across distributed environments. By applying identity-based access controls and continuously monitoring cloud access behavior, NAC ensures that segmentation remains effective even in cloud-native architectures.

Regulatory compliance is another key driver for integrating NAC with network segmentation. Many industries, including healthcare, finance, and government sectors, are required to implement strict access controls to protect sensitive data. Regulations such as HIPAA, PCI DSS, and GDPR mandate network segmentation to isolate sensitive information from general network traffic. NAC helps organizations achieve compliance by enforcing access restrictions, logging authentication attempts, and generating audit reports that demonstrate adherence to regulatory requirements. By implementing NAC-based segmentation, organizations can reduce the risk of compliance violations and ensure that sensitive data remains protected at all times.

Automating NAC policies improves both security and operational efficiency by reducing the complexity of managing segmentation rules. Manual access control configurations are prone to human error and can lead to inconsistencies in security enforcement. Modern NAC solutions leverage artificial intelligence and machine learning to analyze network behavior, detect anomalies, and dynamically adjust access policies based on real-time risk assessments. If a user exhibits unusual behavior, such as attempting to access restricted resources from an unfamiliar location, NAC can trigger an automatic security response, such as requiring additional authentication or temporarily blocking access. Automation enhances the scalability of NAC-based segmentation while ensuring that security policies remain adaptive and responsive to evolving threats.

Organizations implementing NAC-based segmentation must also consider the challenges of deployment and integration with existing network infrastructure. Legacy networks may lack the necessary authentication mechanisms or integration capabilities to support NAC, requiring upgrades to network hardware and software. Compatibility with existing firewalls, identity management systems, and endpoint security solutions is essential for ensuring seamless policy enforcement. A phased deployment approach, starting with pilot implementations and gradually expanding to full-scale segmentation, helps organizations minimize disruption while optimizing NAC-based security policies.

As cyber threats become more sophisticated and attack surfaces continue to expand, NAC and network segmentation remain essential for protecting enterprise networks. By enforcing strict access controls, verifying device compliance, and dynamically adjusting segmentation policies, NAC provides organizations with a powerful defense against unauthorized access and lateral movement threats. When combined with Zero Trust principles, microsegmentation, and cloud security frameworks, NAC-based segmentation enhances both security resilience and network agility, ensuring that organizations can adapt to emerging security challenges while maintaining secure, segmented network environments.

Role of Identity and Access Management (IAM)

Identity and Access Management (IAM) plays a critical role in securing modern networks by ensuring that only authorized users and devices can access specific resources. As organizations expand their digital infrastructure across cloud environments, remote workforces, and distributed applications, IAM has become an essential security framework for managing access controls, enforcing authentication policies, and preventing unauthorized access. By integrating IAM with network segmentation strategies, businesses can create a more secure and efficient IT environment that minimizes attack surfaces, reduces security risks, and enhances regulatory compliance.

Traditional access control methods relied on static credentials such as usernames and passwords to grant or deny access. However, this approach has proven inadequate in today's threat landscape, where cybercriminals frequently exploit weak or stolen credentials to gain unauthorized access to sensitive data. IAM addresses these challenges by implementing multi-factor authentication (MFA), single sign-on (SSO), and role-based access control (RBAC) to enforce stricter security policies. By requiring multiple forms of verification before granting access, IAM ensures that only legitimate users can interact with critical network resources.

The principle of least privilege (PoLP) is a core concept in IAM that aligns closely with network segmentation. Under PoLP, users and devices are granted only the minimum level of access required to perform their functions. This approach prevents unauthorized users from accessing sensitive systems and limits the potential damage caused by compromised credentials. IAM solutions enforce PoLP by assigning specific permissions based on user roles, job functions, and contextual factors such as location and device security posture. By integrating IAM with network segmentation, organizations can ensure that access is granted on a need-to-know basis, reducing the risk of lateral movement by attackers.

IAM also plays a crucial role in enforcing Zero Trust security models, which operate on the assumption that no entity should be trusted by default, whether inside or outside the network perimeter. In a Zero Trust environment, access is continuously verified based on user identity, device health, and behavioral analytics. IAM enables this by incorporating risk-based authentication, real-time monitoring, and identity verification mechanisms. Instead of relying on static trust relationships, IAM ensures that every access request is evaluated dynamically, reducing the likelihood of unauthorized access and insider threats.

Cloud environments have introduced new complexities in identity and access management. Unlike traditional on-premises networks, cloud infrastructures require dynamic access controls that adapt to changing workloads, user behaviors, and multi-cloud architectures. IAM solutions for cloud environments provide centralized identity management, allowing organizations to enforce consistent access policies across multiple cloud platforms. By integrating IAM with cloud security frameworks, businesses can maintain visibility over user activities, enforce least-privilege access, and ensure compliance with data protection regulations. Cloud-native IAM features such as identity federation, conditional access policies, and API security help organizations manage access across distributed environments effectively.

Role-based access control (RBAC) and attribute-based access control (ABAC) are two common IAM models that enhance network segmentation. RBAC assigns permissions based on predefined roles, ensuring that users only have access to resources relevant to their job functions. For example, an HR employee may be granted access to payroll data but restricted from IT administrative functions. ABAC takes access control a step further by considering additional attributes such as device type, location, time of access, and security posture. This granular approach allows organizations to enforce dynamic access policies that adapt to real-time security conditions, preventing unauthorized access while allowing legitimate activities to proceed.

IAM also supports identity governance and compliance initiatives by providing organizations with detailed audit trails, access logs, and policy enforcement mechanisms. Many regulatory frameworks, including GDPR, HIPAA, and PCI DSS, require businesses to maintain strict access controls and ensure that sensitive data is only accessible to authorized individuals. IAM solutions automate compliance reporting, track user activities, and generate audit logs that demonstrate adherence to security policies. By integrating IAM with network segmentation, organizations can enforce compliance-driven segmentation policies that restrict access to regulated data and prevent security breaches.

Privileged Access Management (PAM) is a specialized IAM component that focuses on securing access to high-risk accounts, such as system administrators, database managers, and cloud infrastructure operators. Privileged accounts have elevated permissions that, if compromised, could lead to severe security breaches. PAM solutions enforce strict access controls for privileged users, requiring additional authentication steps, session monitoring, and just-in-time access provisioning. By integrating PAM with network segmentation, organizations can isolate privileged accounts from general user environments, reducing the risk of privilege escalation attacks and insider threats.

IAM extends beyond human users to include machine identities, service accounts, and API access management. In modern IT environments, applications, cloud services, and automated processes frequently interact with one another, requiring secure authentication mechanisms. IAM solutions provide identity verification for non-human entities, ensuring that only trusted applications and services can access network resources. API security, certificate-based authentication, and identity federation help organizations prevent unauthorized machine-to-machine communications, securing automated workflows and cloud integrations.

The integration of IAM with artificial intelligence (AI) and machine learning (ML) enhances identity protection and access control. AI-driven IAM solutions analyze user behavior, detect anomalies, and flag suspicious access attempts in real time. By leveraging ML algorithms, IAM can identify patterns that indicate credential abuse, phishing attacks, or insider threats. Automated risk scoring allows IAM systems to enforce adaptive access controls, such as requiring additional authentication for high-risk activities or blocking access entirely when a security threat is detected. This intelligent approach strengthens network segmentation by dynamically adjusting access permissions based on evolving security risks.

As organizations continue to adopt hybrid and remote work models, IAM plays a vital role in securing remote access and endpoint security. Employees, contractors, and third-party vendors frequently access corporate networks from various devices and locations, increasing the risk of unauthorized access. IAM solutions enforce secure remote access policies by verifying user identities, enforcing device compliance checks, and implementing conditional access rules. By integrating IAM with Zero Trust Network Access (ZTNA), organizations can segment remote users from critical resources, ensuring that access is granted only under secure conditions.

IAM also enhances user experience by streamlining authentication processes while maintaining security. Single sign-on (SSO) enables users to access multiple applications with a single authentication event, reducing password fatigue and minimizing the risk of credential reuse attacks. Adaptive authentication dynamically adjusts security requirements based on user behavior, ensuring a seamless yet secure login experience. By balancing security and usability, IAM solutions help organizations maintain productivity while enforcing strict access controls across segmented networks.

The future of IAM is evolving toward decentralized identity management, where users have greater control over their digital identities. Emerging technologies such as blockchain-based identity verification and self-sovereign identity (SSI) are transforming how organizations manage authentication and access control. Decentralized IAM solutions reduce reliance on centralized identity providers, enhancing privacy and reducing the risk of identity theft. As organizations adopt new identity management technologies, the integration of IAM with network segmentation will continue to play a crucial role in securing digital ecosystems and preventing unauthorized access.

By implementing robust IAM strategies, organizations can strengthen network segmentation, enforce least-privilege access, and reduce the risk of cyber threats. As identity-related attacks, such as credential theft and account takeovers, become more prevalent, IAM solutions provide the necessary tools to authenticate users, monitor access activities, and enforce security policies dynamically. The combination of IAM, Zero Trust principles, and network segmentation creates a multi-layered security framework that ensures secure access to critical resources while preventing unauthorized movements within the network.

Microsegmentation in Cloud Environments

Microsegmentation in cloud environments is a critical security strategy that allows organizations to enforce granular access controls between workloads, applications, and services. Unlike traditional network segmentation, which relies on VLANs and firewalls to separate network traffic, microsegmentation operates at the workload level, ensuring that only authorized communication is permitted between different cloud resources. As businesses continue migrating to cloud infrastructures, securing workloads dynamically while maintaining operational efficiency has become increasingly important.

Microsegmentation provides a solution by enabling precise security policies that adapt to the dynamic nature of cloud environments.

Cloud computing has introduced new security challenges that traditional segmentation methods cannot adequately address. In on-premises environments, network boundaries are well-defined, and security teams have greater control over traffic flows. However, in cloud environments, workloads are often distributed across multiple regions, virtual networks, and cloud providers. Traditional perimeter-based security models fail to provide the necessary visibility and control over east-west traffic, the internal communication between cloud resources. Microsegmentation mitigates this risk by applying identity-based policies that restrict workload communication based on predefined security rules, preventing unauthorized access and limiting the lateral movement of threats.

One of the primary advantages of microsegmentation in cloud environments is the ability to enforce Zero Trust principles. Zero Trust operates on the assumption that no entity, whether inside or outside the network, should be inherently trusted. Every communication request must be authenticated, authorized, and continuously verified. Microsegmentation aligns with this approach by ensuring that cloud workloads can only communicate with explicitly authorized counterparts. Even if an attacker gains access to a compromised cloud instance, microsegmentation prevents them from moving laterally to other workloads, significantly reducing the attack surface.

Cloud-native security solutions have integrated microsegmentation capabilities to address the evolving security landscape. Many cloud service providers offer built-in microsegmentation features, such as AWS Security Groups, Azure Network Security Groups (NSGs), and Google Cloud firewall policies. These tools enable organizations to define security rules that govern how workloads interact with each other within a cloud environment. Unlike traditional firewall-based segmentation, which relies on static rules and IP addresses, cloud-native microsegmentation policies are often identity-based, leveraging workload metadata, tags, and application-level attributes to enforce security controls dynamically.

Workload identity and tagging play a crucial role in microsegmentation strategies for cloud environments. Instead of relying solely on IP addresses, which can frequently change in dynamic cloud infrastructures, microsegmentation policies are applied based on workload identities. By tagging cloud instances, virtual machines, and containers with specific attributes, security teams can create segmentation rules that follow workloads regardless of where they are deployed. This approach ensures that segmentation policies remain consistent across multi-cloud and hybrid environments, even as workloads scale up or down.

Containerized environments and Kubernetes clusters introduce additional complexities in implementing microsegmentation. Traditional network security models are not designed to handle the ephemeral nature of containers, where workloads are continuously created, scaled, and destroyed. Kubernetes provides built-in network segmentation features, such as Network Policies, which allow administrators to define rules that control how pods communicate with each other. Microsegmentation enhances Kubernetes security by enforcing least-privilege access controls between containers, preventing unauthorized interactions, and reducing the impact of potential security breaches.

Hybrid cloud architectures require consistent microsegmentation policies that extend across both on-premises and cloud environments. Many organizations operate in hybrid models, where workloads are distributed between data centers and cloud platforms. Maintaining consistent security policies across these environments is challenging due to differences in network configurations, security controls, and access management systems. Microsegmentation solutions that integrate with hybrid cloud architectures enable organizations to enforce uniform security policies, ensuring that workloads remain protected regardless of their deployment location.

Automation and orchestration are essential components of microsegmentation in cloud environments. Managing segmentation policies manually in large-scale cloud infrastructures is impractical, as workloads frequently change based on demand, resource availability, and business requirements. Automation tools, such as infrastructure-as-code (IaC) frameworks and cloud security platforms, enable organizations to define microsegmentation policies programmatically. By integrating with CI/CD pipelines, security policies can be automatically applied as new workloads are deployed, reducing the risk of human error and ensuring that security remains consistent across dynamic cloud environments.

Threat detection and response capabilities are significantly enhanced through microsegmentation. By limiting workload communication to only necessary interactions, microsegmentation reduces the attack surface and makes it easier to detect anomalies. Security teams can monitor east-west traffic within cloud environments and identify suspicious behavior, such as unauthorized access attempts, lateral movement, or unusual data transfers. Integrating microsegmentation with cloud security monitoring tools, such as SIEM (Security Information and Event Management) and XDR (Extended Detection and Response) solutions, provides real-time visibility into potential security incidents and enables rapid response to mitigate threats.

Regulatory compliance is another critical factor driving the adoption of microsegmentation in cloud environments. Many industries are subject to strict data protection regulations that require organizations to implement access controls, data segmentation, and security monitoring. Regulations such as GDPR, HIPAA, PCI DSS, and SOC 2 mandate that sensitive data must be isolated and protected from unauthorized access. Microsegmentation helps organizations achieve compliance by enforcing security policies that restrict access to regulated data, logging all access attempts, and providing detailed audit trails for security reviews. By segmenting workloads based on compliance requirements, businesses can reduce regulatory risks and avoid costly penalties.

Despite its benefits, implementing microsegmentation in cloud environments comes with challenges. One of the primary challenges is defining effective segmentation policies without disrupting legitimate business processes. Overly restrictive policies can break application dependencies, causing performance issues and operational inefficiencies. Security teams must conduct thorough network traffic analysis to understand normal workload interactions before implementing segmentation rules. By leveraging machine learning and behavioral analytics, organizations can identify baseline traffic patterns and generate segmentation policies that balance security with operational needs.

Another challenge is ensuring visibility across distributed cloud environments. Many organizations operate in multi-cloud architectures, where workloads are deployed across different cloud providers with varying security controls. Managing microsegmentation across these environments requires centralized visibility and policy enforcement. Cloud security posture management (CSPM) tools and cloud-native security platforms help organizations gain insight into workload interactions, enforce segmentation policies consistently, and detect security misconfigurations. Ensuring visibility across hybrid and multi-cloud environments is essential for maintaining an effective microsegmentation strategy.

The future of microsegmentation in cloud environments is expected to incorporate advanced technologies such as artificial intelligence and machine learning. AI-driven security analytics can analyze vast amounts of cloud traffic data to detect patterns, predict potential threats, and recommend segmentation policies. Adaptive microsegmentation solutions will leverage AI to automatically adjust security controls in response to emerging threats, improving network resilience and reducing the need for manual intervention. As cloud infrastructures continue to evolve, organizations will increasingly rely on intelligent automation to manage microsegmentation policies effectively.

Organizations that implement microsegmentation in cloud environments gain significant security advantages, including reduced attack surfaces, enhanced threat containment, improved regulatory compliance, and better overall visibility into workload interactions. By leveraging cloud-native security features, identity-based policies, automation tools, and real-time threat detection, businesses can enforce robust microsegmentation strategies that protect cloud workloads from modern cyber threats. As security threats become more sophisticated, microsegmentation will remain a fundamental pillar of cloud security, ensuring that workloads remain secure, isolated, and resilient against unauthorized access and cyberattacks.

Best Practices for Cloud Segmentation

Cloud segmentation is an essential security practice that enables organizations to control access, restrict communication between workloads, and minimize the attack surface in cloud environments. Unlike traditional on-premises networks, cloud infrastructures are highly dynamic, with workloads constantly being created, moved, and scaled across multiple regions and providers. Without proper segmentation, unauthorized users, malware, or misconfigured resources can lead to significant security breaches. Implementing effective cloud segmentation requires a combination of well-defined policies, automation, identity-based controls, and continuous monitoring to ensure that cloud workloads remain secure, compliant, and optimized for performance.

One of the most fundamental best practices for cloud segmentation is adopting a Zero Trust approach. Zero Trust operates on the principle that no entity, whether inside or outside the network, should be trusted by default. Every access request must be authenticated, authorized, and continuously verified based on context, identity, and risk level. Cloud segmentation aligns with Zero Trust by ensuring that workloads, applications, and users are only allowed to communicate when explicitly permitted. This prevents unauthorized lateral movement and reduces the risk of data breaches caused by compromised accounts or misconfigured cloud resources.

Defining clear segmentation policies is a crucial step in securing cloud environments. Organizations must categorize workloads based on their function, sensitivity, and compliance requirements. High-risk workloads, such as databases containing sensitive customer data, should be isolated from general application servers, development environments, and public-facing web services. Security teams must establish granular access control policies that govern how different segments interact, ensuring that critical assets remain protected from unauthorized access. By implementing strict network segmentation rules, organizations can prevent unauthorized users from accessing high-value workloads and reduce the potential impact of security incidents.

Identity-based segmentation enhances security by ensuring that access controls are enforced based on user roles, device health, and contextual factors. Unlike traditional network segmentation, which relies on IP addresses and static rules, identity-based segmentation dynamically grants access based on authentication and authorization policies. Cloud providers offer identity and access management (IAM) solutions that enable organizations to define role-based access controls (RBAC) and attribute-based access controls (ABAC) for cloud workloads. By integrating IAM with cloud segmentation strategies, organizations can ensure that only authenticated users and services can interact with specific resources.

Implementing workload tagging and metadata-based policies is another best practice for cloud segmentation. Cloud environments frequently change, and manually managing segmentation rules for every workload is impractical. Organizations can use tags and labels to group workloads by department, security level, or application function, enabling automated enforcement of segmentation policies. For example, security teams can create policies that automatically apply firewall rules, network security groups, or microsegmentation controls based on workload tags. This ensures that security policies remain consistent and adaptable to the dynamic nature of cloud environments.

Using microsegmentation within cloud networks provides an additional layer of protection by enforcing least-privilege access between workloads. Microsegmentation limits communication between cloud instances, containers, and virtual machines to only what is necessary for business operations. Instead of allowing broad communication between all workloads in a cloud environment, microsegmentation creates highly specific security policies that restrict unauthorized traffic. This prevents attackers from moving laterally if they gain access to a compromised workload. Cloud-native security solutions, such as AWS Security Groups, Azure Network Security Groups (NSGs), and Kubernetes Network Policies, enable organizations to enforce microsegmentation without relying on traditional perimeter defenses.

Automation and orchestration play a key role in maintaining effective cloud segmentation. Given the scale and complexity of cloud environments, manually managing segmentation policies is not feasible. Organizations should leverage infrastructure-as-code (IaC) frameworks, such as Terraform and AWS CloudFormation, to define and enforce segmentation policies automatically. Security orchestration and automation platforms (SOAR) can further enhance cloud segmentation by dynamically adjusting access controls in response to detected threats. Automating segmentation policies reduces the risk of human error, ensures consistency across cloud environments, and enables rapid response to security incidents.

Continuous monitoring and real-time visibility are essential for detecting security gaps and enforcing segmentation policies effectively. Organizations must deploy cloud security posture management (CSPM) tools to identify misconfigurations, unauthorized access attempts, and policy violations. Cloud-native monitoring solutions, such as AWS CloudTrail, Azure Security Center, and Google Cloud Security Command Center, provide detailed insights into network activity, enabling security teams to detect anomalies and take corrective actions. By continuously monitoring cloud traffic and enforcing segmentation rules, organizations can maintain a strong security posture and reduce the risk of cloud-based attacks.

Protecting cloud environments from misconfigurations requires regular audits and compliance checks. Many cloud security incidents result from misconfigured access controls, excessive permissions, or improperly segmented workloads. Organizations should conduct routine security assessments to ensure that segmentation policies align with industry best practices and regulatory requirements. Compliance frameworks such as GDPR, HIPAA, PCI DSS, and SOC 2 require organizations to implement strict access controls and data protection measures. Automated compliance tools can scan cloud environments for segmentation misconfigurations and provide recommendations for remediation.

Securing hybrid and multi-cloud architectures requires a unified segmentation strategy that extends across different cloud providers and on-premises networks. Many organizations operate in multi-cloud environments, using services from AWS, Azure, and Google Cloud simultaneously. Ensuring consistent segmentation policies across these platforms can be challenging due to differences in security controls and network configurations. Cloud security solutions that provide centralized policy management enable organizations to enforce consistent segmentation rules regardless of where workloads are deployed. By standardizing segmentation policies across hybrid and multi-cloud environments, organizations can prevent security inconsistencies and reduce operational complexity.

Encrypting data in transit and at rest adds another layer of security to cloud segmentation. Even with strict segmentation policies in place, data must be protected from unauthorized access during transmission between cloud workloads. Organizations should implement encryption protocols such as TLS for securing network traffic and AES for encrypting stored data. Secure key management practices, such as using cloud-based key management systems (KMS), ensure that encryption keys are protected from unauthorized access. Combining encryption with segmentation ensures that even if an attacker gains access to a cloud segment, they cannot extract sensitive data without the proper decryption keys.

Incident response planning should be an integral part of cloud segmentation strategies. Despite strong security controls, cloud environments remain potential targets for cyber threats. Organizations must develop incident response playbooks that outline how to detect, contain, and mitigate security breaches within segmented cloud environments. Automated response mechanisms, such as isolating compromised workloads, revoking access privileges, and triggering security alerts, help minimize the impact of security incidents. By integrating segmentation with incident response workflows, organizations can improve their ability to contain and remediate security threats in real time.

As cloud environments continue to evolve, implementing best practices for cloud segmentation is essential for maintaining security, compliance, and operational efficiency. By adopting Zero Trust principles, enforcing identity-based access controls, leveraging automation, and continuously monitoring network activity, organizations can create a robust cloud segmentation framework that minimizes security risks. With the increasing complexity of cloud infrastructures, the ability to segment workloads effectively will remain a critical component of modern cybersecurity strategies. Organizations that prioritize segmentation will be better equipped to protect sensitive data, prevent unauthorized access, and maintain a secure cloud computing environment.

Segmentation in Hybrid and Multi-Cloud Setups

Segmentation in hybrid and multi-cloud setups is an essential security practice that helps organizations manage access controls, isolate workloads, and prevent unauthorized lateral movement. As enterprises increasingly rely on hybrid environments that combine on-premises data centers with public and private cloud services, traditional network security models must evolve to address new challenges. Segmentation ensures that workloads remain secure, even as they move between different cloud providers, data centers, and edge computing environments. By implementing effective segmentation strategies, organizations can reduce attack surfaces, enforce compliance, and maintain consistent security policies across complex infrastructures.

Hybrid cloud environments integrate on-premises infrastructure with cloud services, allowing organizations to extend their data centers while maintaining control over critical workloads. In a hybrid setup, segmentation is necessary to separate sensitive corporate data from cloud-hosted applications, ensuring that security policies remain consistent across different environments. Segmentation enables organizations to enforce strict access controls, preventing unauthorized users from accessing critical systems and reducing the risk of data breaches. A well-designed hybrid cloud segmentation strategy provides visibility into traffic flows, ensures compliance with security policies, and minimizes the risk of lateral movement in the event of a breach.

Multi-cloud architectures involve the use of multiple cloud providers to distribute workloads, applications, and services. While multi-cloud setups offer increased flexibility, scalability, and redundancy, they also introduce security complexities due to the differences in each provider's network architecture, security controls, and access management systems. Segmentation in multi-cloud environments ensures that workloads remain isolated based on business requirements, security policies, and compliance regulations. Organizations must establish a segmentation framework that defines communication rules between cloud workloads, preventing misconfigurations that could expose sensitive data to unauthorized entities.

One of the primary challenges in hybrid and multi-cloud segmentation is ensuring consistent policy enforcement across different environments. Each cloud provider offers its own set of networking tools and security controls, making it difficult to implement uniform segmentation policies. AWS, Azure, and Google Cloud provide cloud-native security features such as Security Groups, Network Security Groups (NSGs), and VPC firewalls, but these tools are not always interoperable. Organizations must adopt security solutions that provide centralized policy management, ensuring that segmentation rules are consistently enforced across all cloud providers and on-premises networks. Security orchestration platforms, cloud security posture management (CSPM) tools, and software-defined networking (SDN) solutions help bridge the gap between different cloud environments, providing a unified approach to segmentation.

Identity-based segmentation enhances security in hybrid and multi-cloud setups by granting access based on user identities, device attributes, and contextual factors rather than relying solely on network-based controls. Traditional segmentation methods use IP addresses, VLANs, and subnets to restrict access, but these approaches are less effective in dynamic cloud environments where workloads frequently change locations. Identity and Access Management (IAM) solutions enable organizations to enforce role-based access controls (RBAC) and attribute-based access controls (ABAC) across hybrid and multi-cloud architectures. By integrating IAM with segmentation policies, organizations can ensure that users and applications can only access specific workloads based on predefined security requirements.

Microsegmentation plays a crucial role in securing hybrid and multi-cloud environments by enforcing least-privilege access at the workload level. Unlike traditional segmentation, which operates at the subnet or network layer, microsegmentation applies security policies at a granular level, restricting communication between applications, virtual machines, and containers. This approach ensures that even if an attacker compromises a single workload, they cannot move laterally across the network. Cloud-native microsegmentation solutions use identity-based tagging, application-layer policies, and software-defined controls to isolate workloads, reducing the risk of internal threats and unauthorized access.

Automation is key to maintaining effective segmentation in hybrid and multi-cloud environments. Manually configuring segmentation rules for thousands of cloud workloads and on-premises systems is impractical and prone to human error. Organizations should leverage automation tools such as Infrastructure-as-Code (IaC), security policy orchestration, and AI-driven threat detection to dynamically enforce segmentation policies. Automated workflows can detect changes in cloud environments, adjust access controls in real-time, and respond to security incidents by isolating compromised workloads. Cloud security automation reduces administrative overhead, improves response times, and ensures that segmentation policies remain aligned with evolving security threats.

Visibility and monitoring are essential for detecting security risks and enforcing segmentation policies across hybrid and multi-cloud setups. Without comprehensive visibility, organizations may struggle to identify unauthorized access attempts, misconfigured security groups, or anomalous traffic patterns. Cloud-native monitoring solutions, such as AWS CloudTrail, Azure Monitor, and Google Cloud Security Command Center, provide real-time insights into network activity, allowing security teams to detect and mitigate segmentation violations. Security Information and Event Management (SIEM) platforms, extended detection and response (XDR) solutions, and AI-driven analytics enhance threat detection capabilities by correlating data across multiple cloud providers and on-premises networks.

Compliance and regulatory requirements further emphasize the need for segmentation in hybrid and multi-cloud environments. Many industries must comply with strict data protection regulations, such as the General Data Protection Regulation (GDPR), the Health Insurance Portability and Accountability Act (HIPAA), and the Payment Card Industry Data Security Standard (PCI DSS). These regulations require organizations to enforce strict access controls, isolate sensitive workloads, and maintain detailed audit logs of network activity. Segmentation helps organizations meet compliance requirements by restricting access to regulated data, enforcing encryption policies, and generating reports that demonstrate adherence to security best practices. Automated compliance monitoring tools provide real-time visibility into regulatory compliance status, helping organizations identify and remediate security gaps.

Hybrid and multi-cloud segmentation must also account for secure data transfer between environments. Workloads often need to communicate across different cloud providers and on-premises systems, requiring secure network pathways that prevent data exposure and unauthorized interception. Virtual private networks (VPNs), secure tunnels, and cloud-native encryption protocols, such as Transport Layer Security (TLS), ensure that data remains protected during transmission. Cloud providers offer interconnect services that facilitate secure and high-speed connectivity between different environments, but organizations must enforce strict access controls to prevent unauthorized data transfers between segmented workloads.

Incident response planning is a critical component of hybrid and multi-cloud segmentation. Despite strong segmentation policies, cyber threats continue to evolve, requiring organizations to have a well-defined strategy for detecting, containing, and mitigating security incidents. Automated response mechanisms, such as isolating compromised workloads, revoking access credentials, and generating real-time security alerts, enhance an organization's ability to respond to security breaches. By integrating segmentation with incident response workflows, organizations can contain threats before they escalate, minimizing the impact on critical business operations.

Organizations that successfully implement segmentation in hybrid and multi-cloud environments benefit from improved security, reduced risk exposure, and enhanced compliance. By adopting Zero Trust principles, leveraging automation, enforcing identity-based policies, and continuously monitoring network activity, businesses can create a robust segmentation framework that adapts to the dynamic nature of modern IT environments. As cloud adoption continues to grow, segmentation will remain a foundational security strategy that enables organizations to protect workloads, enforce compliance, and maintain control over distributed infrastructures.

Kubernetes and Container Microsegmentation

Kubernetes and container microsegmentation have become essential security strategies as organizations increasingly adopt containerized applications and microservices architectures. Containers provide flexibility, scalability, and efficiency in modern cloud environments, but they also introduce unique security challenges. Unlike traditional virtual machines or monolithic applications, containers are highly dynamic, frequently created and terminated based on workload demands. This ephemeral nature makes it difficult to enforce consistent security policies using traditional network segmentation methods. Microsegmentation for Kubernetes and containers addresses this challenge by applying fine-grained security controls that restrict communication between individual workloads, reducing attack surfaces and preventing unauthorized lateral movement.

Kubernetes is the leading orchestration platform for managing containerized applications, automating the deployment, scaling, and management of container workloads. However, Kubernetes does not inherently provide strong security isolation between containers. By default, all containers within a Kubernetes cluster can communicate with each other unless explicit restrictions are applied. This open communication model creates security risks, as an attacker who gains access to one compromised container could potentially move laterally across the cluster, accessing sensitive applications, databases, or critical services. Microsegmentation mitigates these risks by implementing strict access controls at the container level, ensuring that only authorized communication is permitted between workloads.

Network policies in Kubernetes serve as a primary mechanism for enforcing microsegmentation. Kubernetes provides native support for network policies that define which pods can communicate with each other based on namespace, labels, and IP addresses. These policies operate at the network layer, enabling administrators to restrict traffic flows between pods, services, and external endpoints. By default, if no network policy is defined, all pods can freely communicate within a cluster. To enforce microsegmentation, organizations must implement explicit network policies that restrict pod-to-pod communication based on security requirements. This approach prevents unauthorized access and reduces the risk of container-based attacks spreading across the cluster.

Label-based segmentation is a key advantage of Kubernetes microsegmentation. Kubernetes assigns metadata labels to pods, allowing administrators to create security policies based on logical groupings rather than static IP addresses. This is particularly useful in dynamic environments where containers are constantly being created, moved, or terminated. By defining security policies based on labels, organizations can enforce access controls consistently, regardless of where containers are deployed within the cluster. For example, administrators can create a policy that allows only frontend pods to communicate with backend services while blocking all other traffic. This level of granularity ensures that microsegmentation adapts to changing workloads without requiring manual network configuration updates.

Service meshes enhance Kubernetes microsegmentation by providing application-layer security controls that extend beyond traditional network policies. A service mesh is an infrastructure layer that manages service-to-service communication, offering features such as encryption, authentication, traffic control, and observability. Popular service mesh solutions, such as Istio, Linkerd, and Consul, provide fine-grained access controls for Kubernetes workloads by enforcing security policies at the application level. Unlike standard Kubernetes network policies that operate at the network layer, service meshes provide deeper security by encrypting traffic, validating service identities, and enabling mutual TLS (mTLS) authentication between microservices. This ensures that even if an attacker gains network access, they cannot intercept or manipulate encrypted service-to-service communication.

Identity-based microsegmentation further strengthens security in Kubernetes environments by enforcing access controls based on workload identity rather than static network attributes. Traditional network segmentation relies on IP addresses and subnets, which are not suitable for containerized environments where workloads are constantly changing. Identity-based segmentation assigns unique cryptographic identities to each workload, allowing security policies to be applied dynamically based on service identity rather than network location. This approach prevents unauthorized services from communicating with sensitive workloads, even if they exist within the same Kubernetes cluster. By integrating identity-based segmentation with Kubernetes microsegmentation, organizations can create Zero Trust environments where access is strictly verified and continuously enforced.

Automating security policy enforcement is critical for maintaining effective Kubernetes microsegmentation. Manual configuration of network policies, firewall rules, and access controls is not feasible in large-scale containerized environments. Organizations should leverage security automation tools, infrastructure-as-code (IaC) frameworks, and policy-as-code solutions to define and enforce segmentation policies programmatically. Tools such as Open Policy Agent (OPA) enable organizations to implement fine-grained access controls using declarative policies that automatically adapt to changes in containerized workloads. By integrating security policies into CI/CD pipelines, organizations can ensure that microsegmentation is applied consistently as new containers are deployed, reducing human error and improving security agility.

Observability and monitoring are essential for detecting and responding to security incidents in Kubernetes environments. Without proper visibility, organizations may struggle to identify unauthorized access attempts, misconfigured policies, or anomalous container behavior. Security teams should deploy monitoring solutions that provide real-time insights into container communication patterns, policy violations, and potential threats. Kubernetes-native security tools, such as Falco, Calico, and Cilium, offer deep visibility into container traffic, helping organizations enforce microsegmentation policies effectively. These tools use behavioral analysis and machine learning to detect unusual activity, enabling rapid response to security threats.

Compliance and regulatory requirements further emphasize the need for Kubernetes microsegmentation. Many industries must adhere to strict security standards that mandate strong access controls, data protection measures, and audit logging. Regulations such as PCI DSS, GDPR, and HIPAA require organizations to segment workloads handling sensitive data to prevent unauthorized access. Kubernetes microsegmentation helps organizations meet compliance requirements by enforcing least-privilege access controls, logging all network activity, and generating audit trails for security reviews. Automating compliance monitoring ensures that segmentation policies remain aligned with regulatory standards, reducing the risk of compliance violations.

Protecting Kubernetes environments from insider threats and privilege escalation attacks requires strict enforcement of role-based access control (RBAC) and workload security policies. Kubernetes RBAC allows administrators to define user permissions at a granular level, restricting access to sensitive workloads based on predefined roles. Organizations should implement least-privilege access principles, ensuring that developers, administrators, and automated services only have access to the resources necessary for their tasks. Combined with microsegmentation, RBAC prevents unauthorized users from gaining control over critical services or modifying security policies.

Securing multi-cluster Kubernetes environments requires consistent segmentation policies that extend across distributed clusters. Many enterprises deploy multiple Kubernetes clusters across different cloud providers, data centers, or edge locations. Ensuring uniform microsegmentation across these environments is challenging due to differences in networking architectures and security configurations. Organizations should use multi-cluster networking solutions that provide centralized policy management and security enforcement across all Kubernetes deployments. By standardizing segmentation policies across multi-cluster environments, organizations can prevent segmentation inconsistencies and maintain a unified security posture.

Future advancements in Kubernetes microsegmentation will likely incorporate artificial intelligence and machine learning to enhance security automation and threat detection. AI-driven security analytics can analyze container behavior, detect anomalies, and automatically adjust microsegmentation policies to respond to emerging threats. Self-learning security models will enable Kubernetes clusters to dynamically adapt their segmentation rules based on real-time network activity, minimizing manual intervention while improving threat mitigation capabilities. As Kubernetes adoption continues to grow, integrating AI-powered microsegmentation solutions will become essential for securing containerized workloads against sophisticated cyber threats.

Organizations implementing Kubernetes and container microsegmentation benefit from increased security, reduced attack surfaces, and improved regulatory compliance. By leveraging Kubernetes network policies, service meshes, identity-based segmentation, and automation tools, businesses can enforce fine-grained security controls that protect containerized workloads from unauthorized access and lateral movement. As cloud-native architectures evolve, microsegmentation will remain a foundational security strategy for securing Kubernetes environments, ensuring that applications remain resilient against emerging cyber threats while maintaining operational flexibility and scalability.

Network Segmentation in Data Centers

Network segmentation in data centers is a crucial security and performance optimization strategy that ensures efficient resource allocation, minimizes attack surfaces, and prevents unauthorized access. As modern data centers become increasingly complex, hosting thousands of virtual machines, containers, and cloud services, traditional flat network architectures are no longer sufficient to protect critical assets. By implementing network segmentation, organizations can enforce strict access controls, enhance operational efficiency, and reduce the risk of cyber threats spreading across their infrastructure.

Data centers house mission-critical applications, databases, and sensitive data, making them prime targets for cyberattacks. Without proper segmentation, an attacker who gains access to a single compromised server can move laterally throughout the network, potentially reaching valuable assets. A well-structured segmentation strategy isolates workloads based on security levels, ensuring that unauthorized access is prevented at multiple layers. This containment approach limits the impact of security breaches and strengthens an organization's overall cybersecurity posture.

One of the fundamental approaches to network segmentation in data centers is physical segmentation. This method involves using dedicated network hardware, such as switches, routers, and firewalls, to create separate network environments for different workloads. Physical segmentation is commonly used in high-security data centers where strict isolation is required between sensitive workloads, such as financial transactions, healthcare records, and government systems. However, physical segmentation can be costly and difficult to scale, as it requires additional hardware for each new segment.

Logical segmentation provides a more flexible and scalable alternative by leveraging software-defined technologies to divide networks into isolated segments. Virtual Local Area Networks (VLANs) are one of the most widely used logical segmentation methods, allowing administrators to create separate network segments within the same physical infrastructure. VLANs enable organizations to segment data center traffic based on function, department, or security requirements, ensuring that different workloads remain isolated. While VLANs offer improved flexibility over physical segmentation, they still require careful configuration to prevent VLAN hopping attacks, where an attacker manipulates VLAN tags to bypass segmentation controls.

Microsegmentation takes data center security a step further by enforcing fine-grained access controls at the workload level. Unlike VLANs, which operate at the network layer, microsegmentation applies security policies at the application and workload level, ensuring that only authorized communication is permitted. This approach is particularly effective in virtualized and cloud-based data centers, where workloads are constantly created, moved, and scaled. Microsegmentation leverages identity-based policies, software-defined networking (SDN), and zero-trust principles to dynamically restrict access between workloads, minimizing the risk of lateral movement in the event of a breach.

Software-defined networking (SDN) has transformed network segmentation in data centers by decoupling network control from underlying hardware. SDN enables centralized policy enforcement, automation, and dynamic segmentation based on real-time traffic patterns and security analytics. Traditional network segmentation required manual configuration of firewalls and ACLs, which could lead to misconfigurations and inconsistencies. With SDN, administrators can define segmentation policies at a centralized controller, which then automatically enforces them across the entire data center. This improves efficiency, reduces operational overhead, and ensures consistent security enforcement across distributed workloads.

Zero Trust security models align closely with network segmentation in data centers by enforcing strict access controls and continuous verification. In a Zero Trust environment, no device, user, or application is automatically trusted, even if it resides within the data center network. Network segmentation supports Zero Trust by ensuring that each workload is isolated and that access is granted based on identity, device posture, and real-time risk assessments. By integrating Zero Trust with network segmentation, organizations can prevent unauthorized access and enforce least-privilege access policies at every layer of the data center.

Performance optimization is another key benefit of network segmentation in data centers. Without proper segmentation, network congestion can become a significant issue, as all workloads share the same traffic lanes. Segmentation allows organizations to optimize traffic flow by prioritizing critical applications and isolating non-essential traffic. This reduces latency, improves application performance, and ensures that high-priority workloads receive the necessary bandwidth. Load balancing, quality of service (QoS) policies, and intelligent traffic routing further enhance performance by distributing workloads efficiently across segmented environments.

Security monitoring and threat detection play a critical role in maintaining effective network segmentation. Data center administrators must continuously monitor traffic flows, access patterns, and segmentation policies to detect potential security violations. Security information and event management (SIEM) systems, intrusion detection and prevention systems (IDPS), and network traffic analysis tools provide real-time visibility into segmented environments. By integrating segmentation with threat intelligence platforms, organizations can detect anomalous behavior, identify policy violations, and respond to security incidents before they escalate.

Regulatory compliance is a major driver for implementing network segmentation in data centers. Many industries, including finance, healthcare, and government, are subject to strict data protection regulations that require organizations to enforce access controls and isolate sensitive data. Regulations such as PCI DSS, HIPAA, GDPR, and NIST mandate that organizations implement segmentation to prevent unauthorized access to regulated data. By segmenting data center networks, organizations can meet compliance requirements, protect sensitive information, and avoid costly fines associated with non-compliance.

Automation and orchestration are essential for managing network segmentation at scale. Manually configuring segmentation policies across thousands of workloads is not practical in large data centers. Organizations should leverage automation tools, such as policy-based network management, artificial intelligence-driven security analytics, and infrastructure-as-code (IaC) frameworks, to streamline segmentation enforcement. Automated policy orchestration ensures that segmentation rules remain consistent across hybrid and multi-cloud environments, reducing the risk of misconfigurations and improving overall security resilience.

The integration of network segmentation with endpoint security and identity management further enhances data center security. Traditional segmentation methods focused primarily on network boundaries, but modern security strategies extend segmentation to user access controls, endpoint security policies, and workload identity verification. By combining segmentation with IAM solutions, organizations can enforce access restrictions based on user roles, device compliance, and contextual risk factors. This approach ensures that only authorized users and devices can interact with specific workloads, reducing the risk of insider threats and credential-based attacks.

Future advancements in network segmentation for data centers will likely incorporate machine learning and artificial intelligence to improve security automation and threat detection. AI-driven security solutions can analyze traffic patterns, detect segmentation anomalies, and dynamically adjust policies to respond to emerging threats. Self-learning security models will enable data centers to adapt their segmentation strategies based on real-time risk assessments, minimizing manual intervention while strengthening security defenses. As cyber threats evolve, AI-powered segmentation solutions will play a critical role in securing data center environments.

Organizations that implement effective network segmentation in data centers benefit from enhanced security, improved performance, and greater compliance with industry regulations. By leveraging a combination of physical and logical segmentation methods, adopting microsegmentation and SDN technologies, and integrating automation and Zero Trust principles, businesses can create a secure and efficient data center architecture. As data centers continue to evolve to support cloud computing, artificial intelligence, and edge computing, network segmentation will remain a fundamental security strategy for protecting critical assets and ensuring the integrity of digital infrastructure.

Endpoint Segmentation Strategies

Endpoint segmentation strategies play a crucial role in modern cybersecurity by restricting and controlling communication between user devices, applications, and network resources. As organizations adopt remote work, bring-your-own-device (BYOD) policies, and cloud-based applications, the traditional perimeter-based security model is no longer sufficient to protect against evolving threats. Endpoints, including laptops, mobile devices, IoT devices, and virtual desktops, have become prime targets for cybercriminals due to their direct access to corporate networks. By implementing endpoint segmentation, organizations can enforce strict access controls, reduce attack surfaces, and prevent lateral movement within the network.

Traditional network segmentation methods focused on dividing internal networks into separate zones using firewalls, VLANs, and access control lists (ACLs). While these methods remain valuable, they do not adequately address the risks associated with endpoints that frequently connect from different locations, use unsecured networks, or interact with cloud-based services. Endpoint segmentation shifts the focus from network-based controls to device-specific access policies, ensuring that each endpoint is isolated and only allowed to communicate with authorized systems. This approach significantly reduces the risk of cyberattacks spreading from compromised devices to other parts of the network.

One of the foundational principles of endpoint segmentation is identity-based access control. Instead of relying solely on IP addresses and subnet restrictions, organizations enforce access policies based on user identity, device health, and contextual factors such as location and time of access. Identity and Access Management (IAM) solutions enable organizations to assign security policies that dynamically adjust based on authentication status, device compliance, and risk assessments. For example, an employee accessing corporate applications from a managed laptop on a secure corporate network may have full access, whereas the same employee using an unmanaged mobile device on a public Wi-Fi network may be restricted to read-only access.

Zero Trust security models align closely with endpoint segmentation by enforcing least-privilege access controls. In a Zero Trust environment, every access request is continuously verified, and no device or user is automatically trusted, regardless of whether they are inside or outside the network perimeter. Endpoint segmentation enforces Zero Trust by ensuring that devices are only granted access to the specific applications and data they need. This minimizes the risk of credential theft, insider threats, and unauthorized lateral movement within the network. Organizations that implement Zero Trust endpoint segmentation reduce their exposure to ransomware, phishing attacks, and malware infections.

Microsegmentation extends endpoint security by applying granular access controls at the application and workload level. Unlike traditional segmentation, which often relies on broad network segments, microsegmentation isolates individual devices and applications, ensuring that unauthorized communication is blocked. Security policies can be enforced using host-based firewalls, endpoint detection and response (EDR) solutions, and software-defined security platforms. This prevents a compromised endpoint from being used as a pivot point to attack critical business systems. For example, if a laptop is infected with malware, microsegmentation policies can prevent it from communicating with corporate databases, limiting the damage of a potential breach.

Dynamic policy enforcement is essential for maintaining effective endpoint segmentation. Static firewall rules and ACLs are not sufficient in environments where endpoints frequently change locations, connect to different networks, and run various applications. Organizations must implement security policies that automatically adapt to changes in endpoint behavior and risk levels. Endpoint security solutions leverage artificial intelligence (AI) and machine learning to analyze real-time traffic patterns, detect anomalies, and enforce dynamic segmentation rules. If an endpoint exhibits suspicious behavior, such as attempting to access unauthorized resources or initiating unexpected outbound connections, automated security policies can immediately isolate the device to prevent further compromise.

Secure remote access is a critical component of endpoint segmentation, especially with the widespread adoption of remote work and cloud-based applications. Traditional VPN-based access models provide broad network access, allowing remote employees to connect to corporate resources without granular security controls. Modern endpoint segmentation strategies replace VPNs with Zero Trust Network Access (ZTNA) solutions, which enforce application-level access based on identity, device posture, and security policies. Unlike traditional VPNs, which grant network-wide access, ZTNA ensures that remote endpoints can only access specific applications and services, reducing the risk of unauthorized access and data leakage.

IoT devices present unique challenges for endpoint segmentation, as many IoT systems lack built-in security controls and cannot support traditional endpoint protection measures. Organizations must implement segmentation policies that isolate IoT devices from critical business applications and sensitive data. Network access control (NAC) solutions help enforce segmentation by dynamically assigning IoT devices to dedicated network segments based on device type, manufacturer, and risk level. For example, security cameras, smart sensors, and industrial control systems should be placed in separate network segments with strict access controls, preventing unauthorized communication with corporate IT systems.

Compliance and regulatory requirements further emphasize the importance of endpoint segmentation in protecting sensitive data. Many industries, including healthcare, finance, and government, must comply with strict data protection regulations that mandate access controls, encryption, and activity logging. Endpoint segmentation helps organizations meet compliance requirements by ensuring that sensitive information is only accessible to authorized users and devices. Security policies enforce least-privilege access, monitor endpoint activity, and generate audit logs for regulatory reporting. Organizations that fail to implement proper endpoint segmentation risk non-compliance, data breaches, and financial penalties.

Endpoint segmentation must also include robust visibility and monitoring to detect unauthorized access attempts and policy violations. Organizations should deploy Security Information and Event Management (SIEM) systems, Endpoint Detection and Response (EDR) solutions, and cloud access security brokers (CASBs) to gain real-time insights into endpoint activity. Continuous monitoring enables security teams to detect suspicious behavior, respond to incidents, and refine segmentation policies based on emerging threats. By integrating endpoint segmentation with security analytics platforms, organizations can proactively mitigate risks before they lead to full-scale security breaches.

Automation and orchestration are essential for managing endpoint segmentation across large and distributed environments. Manually configuring segmentation policies for thousands of endpoints is inefficient and prone to errors. Security teams should use policy-based automation tools that integrate with endpoint security platforms, IAM systems, and cloud security controls. Automated enforcement ensures that segmentation policies remain consistent, adapt to changing threat landscapes, and minimize human intervention. Organizations that leverage AI-driven automation for endpoint segmentation can respond to threats faster, reduce administrative complexity, and maintain stronger security postures.

Future advancements in endpoint segmentation will likely incorporate AI-driven threat intelligence, behavioral analytics, and continuous adaptive risk assessment. AI-powered security solutions will analyze endpoint behavior patterns, detect emerging threats, and dynamically adjust segmentation policies based on risk levels. Adaptive security frameworks will ensure that endpoint segmentation policies evolve in real-time, providing organizations with a proactive approach to endpoint security. As cyber threats become more sophisticated, endpoint segmentation will remain a critical defense mechanism, enabling businesses to protect devices, data, and applications from unauthorized access and cyberattacks.

By implementing endpoint segmentation strategies, organizations can enhance security, reduce attack surfaces, and prevent unauthorized lateral movement within their networks. Identity-based access controls, microsegmentation, dynamic policy enforcement, and AI-driven automation enable businesses to protect their endpoints from cyber threats while maintaining productivity and operational efficiency. As the number of connected devices and cloud-based applications continues to grow, endpoint segmentation will remain a key security strategy in ensuring the integrity and security of enterprise IT environments.

Role of AI and Machine Learning in Microsegmentation

Artificial intelligence and machine learning have become critical components of modern cybersecurity strategies, particularly in microsegmentation. As organizations shift from traditional perimeter-based security models to more granular segmentation approaches, AI and machine learning offer the ability to automate policy enforcement, detect anomalies, and dynamically adjust security rules in response to emerging threats. Microsegmentation is designed to restrict network traffic at the workload level, ensuring that only authorized entities can communicate. However, managing thousands of dynamic rules manually is impractical. AI-driven microsegmentation enables organizations to implement intelligent and adaptive security policies that improve efficiency and reduce human error.

One of the primary advantages of AI and machine learning in microsegmentation is their ability to analyze network behavior in real-time. Traditional segmentation policies rely on predefined rules that are static and may not adapt to changing network conditions. AI and machine learning algorithms continuously monitor traffic patterns, detect anomalies, and refine security policies based on observed behavior. By learning how workloads, applications, and devices interact within the network, AI-driven microsegmentation can identify normal communication patterns and automatically block unauthorized or suspicious traffic. This proactive approach strengthens security by ensuring that segmentation policies evolve alongside the organization's infrastructure.

Automation is a key benefit of integrating AI with microsegmentation. Manually defining and updating segmentation rules across thousands of workloads and cloud environments is not feasible. AI-powered security solutions automate policy creation and enforcement, reducing administrative overhead and ensuring consistency across the network. Machine learning models analyze vast amounts of network data to determine the most effective segmentation policies, eliminating the need for manual rule adjustments. This level of automation enables organizations to deploy microsegmentation at scale without overwhelming security teams with complex configurations and maintenance tasks.

Threat detection and response are significantly improved through AI-driven microsegmentation. Cyber threats are constantly evolving, and attackers are finding new ways to bypass traditional security controls. Machine learning models can detect patterns associated with malicious activity, such as lateral movement, data exfiltration, and privilege escalation attempts. When a deviation from normal network behavior is detected, AI-driven systems can take immediate action by isolating compromised workloads, blocking unauthorized traffic, or alerting security teams. This real-time threat response minimizes the impact of cyberattacks and prevents the spread of malware or ransomware across segmented environments.

Behavioral analysis plays a crucial role in AI-powered microsegmentation. Traditional network segmentation relies on static access control lists (ACLs) and firewall rules that do not account for behavioral changes. AI models analyze user and workload behavior over time, identifying deviations that could indicate a security threat. For example, if an application that typically communicates with only one internal service suddenly starts sending requests to multiple external servers, AI-driven microsegmentation can flag this anomaly and enforce new policies to restrict the suspicious activity. This approach enhances security by dynamically adjusting access controls based on real-time risk assessments.

AI and machine learning improve the accuracy of segmentation policies by reducing false positives and negatives. One of the biggest challenges in implementing microsegmentation is ensuring that legitimate traffic is not mistakenly blocked while unauthorized traffic is effectively restricted. Machine learning models refine segmentation policies based on historical data, continuously improving their accuracy. Over time, AI-driven systems learn which communications are essential for business operations and which are potential security risks. This ensures that segmentation policies are both effective and operationally efficient, reducing the risk of disrupting legitimate workflows.

Cloud environments benefit significantly from AI-driven microsegmentation. As organizations migrate workloads to multi-cloud and hybrid environments, traditional segmentation approaches struggle to keep up with the dynamic nature of cloud computing. AI-based microsegmentation solutions integrate with cloud-native security tools to provide real-time visibility into cloud traffic, enforce identity-based access controls, and automatically adapt to workload changes. This ensures that segmentation policies remain consistent and effective across on-premises data centers, public clouds, and private cloud environments. AI-driven segmentation also helps organizations maintain compliance with cloud security best practices and regulatory requirements.

Endpoint security is enhanced through AI-powered microsegmentation. As remote work and bring-your-own-device (BYOD) policies become more common, securing endpoints has become a top priority. AI-driven segmentation solutions analyze endpoint behavior and apply security policies dynamically, ensuring that compromised devices do not gain unauthorized access to critical systems. Machine learning algorithms assess endpoint risk levels based on factors such as device posture, user behavior, and geolocation, allowing organizations to enforce contextual access controls. This adaptive security model prevents attackers from exploiting endpoint vulnerabilities to move laterally within segmented networks.

Machine learning models also assist in predicting potential security threats before they occur. Traditional security tools react to known threats based on signature-based detection methods, but AI-driven microsegmentation leverages predictive analytics to anticipate attacks. By analyzing historical network traffic and attack trends, machine learning algorithms identify early indicators of compromise and enforce preventative segmentation policies. This proactive security approach reduces the risk of zero-day attacks and advanced persistent threats (APTs) by detecting anomalies before they escalate into full-scale breaches.

Integrating AI with microsegmentation enhances regulatory compliance by automating policy enforcement and audit reporting. Many industries, including healthcare, finance, and government, require strict segmentation policies to protect sensitive data. AI-driven security platforms automatically generate compliance reports, track policy violations, and ensure that segmentation controls align with regulatory frameworks such as GDPR, HIPAA, and PCI DSS. By automating compliance enforcement, organizations reduce the risk of non-compliance penalties and improve their overall security posture.

One of the challenges of implementing AI-driven microsegmentation is ensuring interoperability with existing security infrastructure. Organizations often use a mix of legacy systems, cloud-native security tools, and on-premises firewalls, making seamless integration a complex task. AI-powered security platforms must support open standards, APIs, and security orchestration frameworks to work effectively across diverse environments. Security teams must also ensure that AI-driven segmentation policies align with business requirements, preventing disruptions to legitimate applications and workflows.

As artificial intelligence continues to evolve, future advancements in AI-driven microsegmentation will focus on enhancing real-time decision-making, improving contextual awareness, and increasing automation capabilities. AI-powered security solutions will incorporate self-learning algorithms that continuously refine segmentation policies based on real-time feedback. Additionally, advancements in federated learning will enable AI models to improve security insights without exposing sensitive data, ensuring privacy and compliance. The integration of AI-driven threat intelligence will further enhance microsegmentation by providing real-time insights into emerging attack techniques and enabling organizations to respond proactively.

Organizations that leverage AI and machine learning in microsegmentation gain a significant advantage in securing their networks, reducing operational complexity, and responding to cyber threats in real-time. AI-driven segmentation enhances security by dynamically enforcing policies, detecting anomalies, automating threat response, and improving compliance. As cyber threats become more sophisticated and IT environments grow more complex, the role of AI in microsegmentation will continue to expand, providing organizations with adaptive and intelligent security solutions that protect critical assets from evolving risks.

Traffic Analysis for Effective Segmentation

Traffic analysis plays a critical role in designing and maintaining effective network segmentation strategies. By examining network traffic patterns, organizations can identify legitimate communication flows, detect anomalies, and enforce security policies that restrict unauthorized access. Without comprehensive traffic analysis, segmentation efforts may be ineffective, leaving gaps that attackers can exploit. Understanding how data moves within the network, between applications, and across different environments enables security teams to create precise segmentation policies that enhance security while maintaining operational efficiency.

One of the primary goals of traffic analysis in segmentation is to gain visibility into how different systems communicate. Many organizations operate complex IT infrastructures that include cloud services, data centers, on-premises networks, and remote endpoints. Without a clear understanding of network traffic flows, segmentation policies may be too broad, allowing excessive access, or too restrictive, disrupting critical business operations. Traffic analysis provides insight into which devices, applications, and users need to communicate, enabling security teams to define segmentation rules that accurately reflect business needs.

Packet inspection is a fundamental technique used in traffic analysis to examine the contents of network packets. Traditional network monitoring tools analyze packet headers to determine the source, destination, protocol, and port number associated with a given transmission. Deep packet inspection (DPI) goes further by analyzing packet payloads to identify specific applications, file types, and user activities. DPI helps organizations enforce segmentation policies by ensuring that only authorized applications and services communicate within specific network segments. By identifying patterns in packet data, security teams can detect potential security threats, such as unauthorized file transfers or malware communication attempts.

Flow-based traffic analysis provides another valuable method for monitoring network activity and supporting segmentation efforts. Instead of inspecting individual packets, flow analysis examines traffic patterns over time to understand communication trends. Technologies such as NetFlow, IPFIX, and sFlow collect metadata about network flows, including source and destination addresses, traffic volume, and duration. This data helps security teams establish baselines for normal network behavior and detect deviations that may indicate security incidents. Flow analysis is particularly useful in identifying unexpected communication between network segments, such as a workstation attempting to access a restricted server.

Machine learning and artificial intelligence (AI) enhance traffic analysis by identifying patterns and anomalies in large volumes of network data. AI-driven traffic analysis solutions can recognize normal communication behaviors and flag deviations that suggest potential threats. These solutions can automatically adjust segmentation policies based on real-time observations, ensuring that security controls remain effective without manual intervention. For example, if a machine learning model detects a sudden increase in traffic between two segments that do not typically interact, it can trigger an alert or dynamically restrict access. AI-driven traffic analysis improves the accuracy of segmentation policies and reduces the risk of human error in configuring security rules.

Behavioral analytics further strengthens traffic analysis by examining how users, devices, and applications interact over time. By tracking behavioral patterns, security teams can distinguish between legitimate traffic and suspicious activity. For example, an employee logging into a corporate system from a known location during business hours represents a normal pattern, while the same credentials being used from an unfamiliar country in the middle of the night may indicate a compromised account. Integrating behavioral analytics with segmentation policies enables organizations to enforce dynamic access controls that adapt to real-time security risks.

Cloud environments present unique challenges for traffic analysis and segmentation. Unlike traditional on-premises networks, cloud-based infrastructures are highly dynamic, with workloads constantly being created, modified, or terminated. Cloud-native traffic analysis tools, such as AWS VPC Flow Logs, Azure Network Watcher, and Google Cloud VPC Flow Logs, provide visibility into cloud traffic flows, helping security teams define appropriate segmentation policies. By analyzing cloud traffic, organizations can enforce identity-based access controls, detect misconfigurations, and prevent unauthorized communication between cloud workloads. Cloud traffic analysis also helps organizations ensure compliance with security standards by monitoring data flows and enforcing regulatory requirements.

Encrypted traffic presents both opportunities and challenges for traffic analysis in segmentation. Many modern applications use Transport Layer Security (TLS) to encrypt data in transit, protecting sensitive information from interception. However, encryption also makes it more difficult for security tools to inspect traffic for potential threats.

Organizations must implement strategies for analyzing encrypted traffic without compromising security or performance. Techniques such as SSL/TLS decryption, encrypted traffic fingerprinting, and metadata analysis allow security teams to monitor encrypted communications while preserving privacy. Properly managing encrypted traffic is essential for enforcing segmentation policies that prevent unauthorized data exchanges while ensuring regulatory compliance.

Segmentation effectiveness depends on continuous monitoring and policy adjustments based on traffic analysis insights. Static segmentation policies may become outdated as network conditions change, leading to security gaps or operational inefficiencies. Continuous traffic monitoring enables organizations to refine segmentation rules in response to new application deployments, user behavior changes, and evolving threat landscapes. Security teams should regularly review traffic data, assess segmentation effectiveness, and update policies to align with business requirements. Automated policy enforcement tools streamline this process by applying real-time traffic insights to segmentation controls.

Threat intelligence integration enhances traffic analysis by providing contextual information about known attack vectors, malicious IP addresses, and emerging cyber threats. Security teams can use threat intelligence feeds to identify suspicious traffic patterns that indicate potential attacks. For example, if traffic analysis detects outbound connections to a known command-and-control server, segmentation policies can be adjusted to block further communication and isolate compromised systems. By integrating threat intelligence with segmentation strategies, organizations can proactively defend against cyber threats and reduce the impact of security incidents.

User and device segmentation benefits from traffic analysis by ensuring that access controls align with security policies. Organizations can classify users and devices based on their roles, risk levels, and behavior patterns. Traffic analysis helps determine whether a device should be placed in a restricted segment, such as a guest network, or granted access to critical systems. Dynamic user segmentation ensures that employees, contractors, and third-party vendors only have access to the resources necessary for their tasks. By continuously analyzing user and device traffic, organizations can enforce segmentation policies that balance security with productivity.

Compliance and regulatory requirements drive the need for traffic analysis in network segmentation. Many industry standards, such as GDPR, HIPAA, PCI DSS, and ISO 27001, require organizations to monitor network traffic, enforce access controls, and maintain audit logs. Traffic analysis ensures that segmentation policies meet compliance requirements by tracking data flows, identifying policy violations, and generating reports for regulatory audits. Automated compliance monitoring tools help organizations maintain segmentation integrity by continuously evaluating traffic patterns and adjusting policies to align with legal requirements.

Incident response and forensics rely on traffic analysis to investigate security breaches and improve segmentation defenses. When a security incident occurs, traffic logs provide valuable insights into how the attack unfolded, which segments were affected, and what corrective actions should be taken. Security teams can use traffic analysis to trace the origin of an attack, identify compromised systems, and refine segmentation policies to prevent future incidents. Effective segmentation, combined with robust traffic analysis, enhances an organization's ability to detect, contain, and mitigate security threats in real time.

Organizations that implement traffic analysis as part of their segmentation strategy gain improved visibility, stronger security controls, and better compliance adherence. By leveraging packet inspection, flow analysis, behavioral analytics, and machine learning, security teams can enforce adaptive segmentation policies that evolve with network conditions. Traffic analysis provides the intelligence needed to refine segmentation rules, detect anomalies, and respond to emerging threats. As cyber threats continue to evolve, organizations must prioritize continuous traffic analysis to ensure that segmentation remains an effective defense mechanism against unauthorized access, lateral movement, and data breaches.

Network Monitoring and Visibility

Network monitoring and visibility are essential components of modern cybersecurity strategies, providing organizations with the ability to detect threats, enforce security policies, and optimize network performance. As IT infrastructures become more complex, with hybrid cloud environments, remote workforces, and an increasing number of connected devices, maintaining visibility into network traffic and security events is more critical than ever. Without proper monitoring, organizations risk falling victim to cyberattacks, operational inefficiencies, and compliance violations. By implementing comprehensive network monitoring and visibility solutions, businesses can proactively detect anomalies, prevent unauthorized access, and ensure seamless network operations.

One of the primary goals of network monitoring is to provide real-time insights into network activity. Organizations must continuously track data flows, user behavior, and system interactions to identify potential security threats or performance issues. Network monitoring solutions collect and analyze network traffic data, allowing security teams to detect unusual activity that may indicate malicious behavior. Advanced monitoring tools leverage artificial intelligence and machine learning to recognize patterns, identify deviations, and generate automated alerts when security incidents occur. Real-time visibility ensures that security teams can respond to threats quickly before they escalate into full-scale breaches.

Packet-level monitoring is a foundational technique for network visibility, capturing and analyzing network packets to provide detailed insights into data transmission. Packet capture solutions allow organizations to inspect network traffic at a granular level, helping detect unauthorized access attempts, data exfiltration, and malware communication. Deep packet inspection (DPI) extends this capability by analyzing packet contents, identifying specific applications, and determining whether traffic complies with security policies. Packet-level monitoring is particularly useful for detecting threats that attempt to evade traditional security controls, such as encrypted malware payloads or covert command-and-control communications.

Flow-based monitoring provides a broader perspective on network activity by analyzing metadata about traffic flows instead of inspecting individual packets. Technologies such as NetFlow, IPFIX, and sFlow collect information about source and destination IP addresses, traffic volume, session duration, and communication protocols. Flow analysis helps security teams understand traffic trends, identify high-risk connections, and detect anomalous behavior. Unlike packet capture, which requires substantial storage and processing power, flow-based monitoring offers scalable visibility into network activity without overwhelming resources. Organizations use flow analytics to establish baselines for normal behavior and quickly detect deviations that may indicate security incidents.

User and entity behavior analytics (UEBA) enhance network visibility by tracking user and device interactions over time. UEBA solutions leverage machine learning algorithms to establish normal behavior patterns for users, endpoints, and applications. When a deviation from expected behavior is detected, such as an employee accessing sensitive data at an unusual time or an endpoint attempting to communicate with unauthorized resources, security teams are alerted to investigate. UEBA helps organizations detect insider threats, compromised credentials, and privilege escalation attempts that traditional security tools may overlook. By continuously analyzing behavior, UEBA provides a proactive approach to threat detection and network monitoring.

Cloud network visibility presents unique challenges due to the dynamic and distributed nature of cloud environments. Unlike traditional on-premises networks, cloud workloads frequently move between data centers, cloud providers, and edge computing environments. Cloud-native monitoring tools, such as AWS CloudTrail, Azure Monitor, and Google Cloud Security Command Center, provide visibility into cloud network traffic, access logs, and security configurations. Cloud network visibility solutions integrate with hybrid cloud architectures to ensure that security teams can track data flows, detect misconfigurations, and enforce segmentation policies across multiple cloud platforms. Without proper cloud visibility, organizations risk losing control over sensitive data and exposing workloads to security vulnerabilities.

Network visibility is also critical for detecting lateral movement within a compromised network. Cybercriminals often use lateral movement techniques to navigate through an organization's infrastructure after gaining initial access. By monitoring internal traffic patterns and identifying unusual communication between network segments, organizations can detect lateral movement before attackers reach high-value assets. Microsegmentation enhances lateral movement detection by restricting unnecessary traffic flows and ensuring that security monitoring tools focus on critical interactions. Security information and event management (SIEM) solutions aggregate network visibility data, allowing analysts to correlate alerts, investigate threats, and respond to security incidents effectively.

Encryption adds complexity to network visibility, as encrypted traffic makes it more difficult for security tools to inspect data flows. While encryption is essential for protecting sensitive information, it can also be exploited by attackers to conceal malicious activity. Organizations must implement encrypted traffic analysis solutions that use machine learning and metadata inspection to detect threats without decrypting sensitive data. SSL/TLS decryption, combined with behavioral analytics, enables security teams to monitor encrypted traffic for signs of cyber threats while maintaining compliance with data protection regulations. Managing encrypted traffic effectively ensures that security teams maintain visibility without compromising privacy.

Endpoint visibility is another crucial aspect of network monitoring, as endpoints often serve as entry points for cyber threats. Security teams must monitor endpoint activity to detect unauthorized access attempts, malware infections, and suspicious behavior. Endpoint detection and response (EDR) solutions provide real-time visibility into endpoint activity, identifying potential threats before they spread across the network. By integrating endpoint monitoring with network visibility tools, organizations can gain a comprehensive understanding of how endpoints interact with network resources and enforce security policies accordingly. Continuous endpoint visibility helps prevent security incidents by detecting and responding to threats at the earliest stages.

Regulatory compliance further underscores the importance of network monitoring and visibility. Many industries are subject to strict data protection regulations, such as the General Data Protection Regulation (GDPR), the Health Insurance Portability and Accountability Act (HIPAA), and the Payment Card Industry Data Security Standard (PCI DSS). These regulations require organizations to maintain detailed logs of network activity, enforce access controls, and implement security monitoring practices to protect sensitive information. Network monitoring solutions provide the visibility needed to meet compliance requirements by generating audit logs, tracking user access, and ensuring that segmentation policies align with regulatory standards. Organizations that fail to maintain network visibility risk compliance violations, legal consequences, and reputational damage.

Automated threat detection and response capabilities enhance network monitoring by reducing the time required to identify and mitigate security incidents. Security orchestration, automation, and response (SOAR) platforms integrate with network visibility tools to automate incident response workflows. When a security alert is triggered, automated playbooks can isolate affected systems, block malicious traffic, and notify security teams for further investigation. AI-driven automation further enhances threat detection by continuously analyzing network behavior and adjusting security policies based on real-time intelligence. Automated threat detection reduces the burden on security teams while improving response times and overall network resilience.

Future advancements in network monitoring and visibility will leverage artificial intelligence, machine learning, and predictive analytics to improve threat detection and response. AI-powered monitoring solutions will analyze vast amounts of network data to identify emerging threats, predict attack patterns, and recommend security actions. Predictive analytics will enable organizations to proactively adjust security policies based on evolving risk factors, reducing the likelihood of cyberattacks before they occur. The integration of AI with network monitoring will enhance security operations, providing security teams with deeper insights, faster detection capabilities, and more effective defense mechanisms against cyber threats.

Organizations that implement comprehensive network monitoring and visibility strategies benefit from improved threat detection, stronger compliance adherence, and optimized network performance. By leveraging packet inspection, flow analysis, UEBA, and cloud-native security tools, businesses can gain real-time insights into network activity and enforce adaptive security policies. Continuous monitoring ensures that organizations can detect and respond to security incidents before they cause significant damage. As cyber threats become more sophisticated, maintaining network visibility will remain a cornerstone of effective cybersecurity, enabling organizations to secure their digital infrastructure while ensuring seamless business operations.

Policy-Based Segmentation

Policy-based segmentation is a security strategy that enforces network access controls through predefined rules and policies rather than relying solely on traditional network boundaries. As IT environments become more complex, spanning on-premises data centers, cloud infrastructures, remote workforces, and IoT devices, policy-based segmentation provides a scalable approach to managing security. By defining access policies based on identity, role, application, or workload attributes, organizations can create dynamic segmentation rules that adapt to changing security needs. Unlike traditional segmentation methods, which rely on static VLANs or IP-based controls, policy-based segmentation enhances flexibility, automation, and security enforcement across distributed environments.

One of the primary advantages of policy-based segmentation is its ability to enforce least-privilege access. This principle ensures that users, devices, and applications can only access the resources necessary for their functions. Instead of assigning broad network permissions, security teams define policies that specify which entities are allowed to communicate and under what conditions. For example, an organization may create policies that allow finance department employees to access financial applications but restrict their access to software development environments. This level of granularity minimizes security risks by reducing unnecessary access and limiting potential attack paths within the network.

Identity-based segmentation plays a crucial role in policy enforcement. Instead of relying solely on network attributes such as IP addresses or subnets, policy-based segmentation integrates with identity and access management (IAM) solutions to enforce role-based access controls. Security policies can be dynamically assigned based on user authentication, device compliance, and contextual factors such as geolocation or time of access. This ensures that segmentation policies remain adaptive and responsive to real-time security conditions. If a user attempts to access sensitive data from an unmanaged device or an unfamiliar location, policy-based segmentation can automatically enforce additional security checks or deny access entirely.

Microsegmentation is a key component of policy-based segmentation, allowing organizations to apply security controls at a granular level. Traditional segmentation methods often rely on broad network zones, making it difficult to isolate workloads effectively. Microsegmentation enforces security policies at the workload or application level, ensuring that only authorized communication is permitted between different entities. This prevents attackers from moving laterally within the network if they compromise a single endpoint. Policy-based microsegmentation solutions dynamically adjust access controls based on real-time risk assessments, preventing unauthorized interactions between applications, servers, and cloud workloads.

Automation enhances the effectiveness of policy-based segmentation by reducing the complexity of managing security rules. Organizations that manually configure segmentation policies face challenges in maintaining consistency, especially in large-scale environments with thousands of endpoints and applications. Security policy orchestration platforms automate the enforcement of segmentation rules, ensuring that policies are consistently applied across the network. By leveraging artificial intelligence and machine learning, these platforms can detect anomalies, suggest policy refinements, and enforce adaptive access controls without requiring manual intervention. Automated policy management helps security teams respond more quickly to emerging threats and maintain strong security postures.

Cloud environments benefit significantly from policy-based segmentation due to their dynamic nature. Unlike traditional networks, where segmentation is often based on physical infrastructure, cloud environments require software-defined security policies that can be applied across multiple regions and service providers. Cloud-native security tools, such as AWS Security Groups, Azure Network Security Groups (NSGs), and Google Cloud Identity-Aware Proxy (IAP), allow organizations to define policies that govern how workloads communicate. Policy-based segmentation ensures that cloud workloads remain isolated and that security controls follow workloads as they move between different cloud environments. This approach prevents misconfigurations that could expose sensitive data to unauthorized access.

Regulatory compliance drives the adoption of policy-based segmentation by ensuring that organizations meet security standards and data protection requirements. Many industries, including finance, healthcare, and government, must enforce strict access controls to protect sensitive information. Regulations such as GDPR, HIPAA, and PCI DSS require organizations to segment networks to limit access to sensitive data and maintain detailed audit logs of access attempts. Policy-based segmentation simplifies compliance by automating access controls, logging security events, and ensuring that policies align with regulatory requirements. By defining segmentation policies based on compliance needs, organizations can reduce the risk of data breaches and regulatory penalties.

Visibility and monitoring play an essential role in policy-based segmentation, allowing security teams to track access patterns and detect policy violations. Without proper visibility, organizations may struggle to enforce segmentation effectively, leading to security gaps or operational disruptions. Network security platforms provide real-time insights into policy enforcement, allowing administrators to identify misconfigured rules, unauthorized access attempts, and potential security threats. Security Information and Event Management (SIEM) solutions, endpoint detection and response (EDR) platforms, and cloud security posture management (CSPM) tools enhance visibility by providing centralized monitoring of segmentation policies across hybrid and multi-cloud environments.

The integration of policy-based segmentation with Zero Trust security models further strengthens network defenses. Zero Trust operates on the principle that no entity should be automatically trusted, requiring continuous verification before granting access. Policy-based segmentation enforces Zero Trust by ensuring that every access request is evaluated against security policies before being approved. Organizations implementing Zero Trust architectures can leverage policy-based segmentation to dynamically enforce authentication, authorization, and least-privilege access controls. This reduces the risk of insider threats, credential theft, and lateral movement attacks by restricting access based on real-time risk assessments.

Endpoint security is another critical aspect of policy-based segmentation. With the rise of remote work and bring-your-own-device (BYOD) policies, organizations must ensure that endpoints connecting to corporate networks comply with security policies. Policy-based segmentation allows organizations to enforce access restrictions based on device compliance, ensuring that unmanaged or compromised devices cannot access sensitive resources. Endpoint security solutions integrate with segmentation policies to enforce contextual access controls, preventing unauthorized devices from communicating with critical applications. This approach helps prevent malware infections, phishing attacks, and ransomware propagation by restricting endpoint interactions within segmented environments.

Incident response and threat mitigation are enhanced through policy-based segmentation by allowing organizations to quickly isolate compromised systems. In the event of a security breach, segmentation policies can dynamically restrict access to affected areas, preventing attackers from escalating privileges or accessing additional resources. Automated incident response workflows integrate with segmentation policies to quarantine compromised endpoints, block malicious traffic, and notify security teams of suspicious activity. This containment approach minimizes the impact of security incidents and enables faster recovery from cyberattacks.

The future of policy-based segmentation will incorporate advanced analytics, artificial intelligence, and machine learning to improve threat detection and security automation. AI-driven security platforms will continuously analyze network activity, adjust segmentation policies based on risk intelligence, and automatically respond to emerging threats. Predictive analytics will help organizations identify potential security risks before they occur, allowing for proactive policy adjustments. As cyber threats evolve, policy-based segmentation will remain a fundamental component of modern security strategies, enabling organizations to protect their networks, applications, and data with greater precision and adaptability.

Organizations that implement policy-based segmentation benefit from enhanced security, improved operational efficiency, and stronger regulatory compliance. By defining access policies based on identity, workload attributes, and contextual factors, businesses can enforce dynamic segmentation rules that adapt to evolving security needs. The integration of automation, Zero Trust principles, and advanced monitoring solutions further strengthens policy-based segmentation, ensuring that organizations can effectively protect their digital assets while maintaining seamless business operations. As IT environments continue to grow in complexity, policy-based segmentation will remain a cornerstone of modern cybersecurity frameworks, providing the flexibility and scalability needed to defend against advanced threats.

Role of SIEM in Microsegmentation

Security Information and Event Management (SIEM) plays a crucial role in microsegmentation by providing real-time monitoring, threat detection, and policy enforcement across segmented environments. As organizations adopt microsegmentation to isolate workloads, limit lateral movement, and enforce least-privilege access, SIEM solutions enhance visibility and security operations by aggregating, analyzing, and correlating security data from multiple sources. SIEM platforms help security teams detect anomalies, identify policy violations, and respond to potential threats before they escalate into full-scale breaches. The integration of SIEM with microsegmentation ensures that segmentation policies remain effective, adaptive, and aligned with evolving security risks.

One of the primary functions of SIEM in microsegmentation is centralized log management and event correlation. Microsegmentation enforces strict access controls between network segments, limiting communication between workloads based on security policies. SIEM collects logs from firewalls, endpoint detection and response (EDR) tools, identity and access management (IAM) systems, and network monitoring solutions, aggregating them into a centralized repository. By analyzing these logs, SIEM identifies security events that may indicate policy violations, unauthorized access attempts, or anomalous behavior within segmented environments. Correlating events from multiple sources provides a comprehensive view of security risks, allowing organizations to refine microsegmentation policies based on real-time insights.

Threat detection is significantly enhanced through SIEM-driven microsegmentation monitoring. Cyber threats, including ransomware, insider threats, and lateral movement attacks, often attempt to bypass traditional security controls by exploiting misconfigured segmentation policies. SIEM solutions leverage advanced analytics and machine learning to detect suspicious activity within microsegmented environments. By analyzing network traffic, user behavior, and system logs, SIEM can identify indicators of compromise (IoCs) that suggest an attacker is attempting to move between segments or escalate privileges. Once detected, SIEM triggers alerts or automated responses to contain threats, preventing security incidents from spreading across the network.

Behavioral analytics within SIEM enhances microsegmentation by detecting deviations from normal traffic patterns. Microsegmentation creates isolated network segments where communication is limited to predefined policies. However, attackers often attempt to exploit segmentation misconfigurations or gain unauthorized access by mimicking legitimate behavior. SIEM platforms use user and entity behavior analytics (UEBA) to establish baselines for normal activity, identifying anomalies that may indicate credential misuse, unauthorized lateral movement, or privilege escalation attempts. If a user or workload exhibits behavior inconsistent with its normal activity, SIEM can flag the event and initiate security responses, such as blocking traffic or enforcing additional authentication measures.

SIEM integration with threat intelligence feeds further strengthens microsegmentation policies. Cyber threats continuously evolve, and attackers frequently use new tactics to bypass security controls. SIEM ingests real-time threat intelligence from external sources, including global threat databases, government cybersecurity agencies, and security vendors. By correlating network activity within segmented environments with known threat indicators, SIEM identifies potential security threats before they cause damage. For example, if an internal workload attempts to communicate with an external IP address associated with a known command-and-control server, SIEM can block the traffic, trigger an alert, and isolate the affected workload within the microsegmented network.

Microsegmentation policy enforcement benefits from SIEM-driven automation and orchestration. Defining and maintaining segmentation rules across complex IT environments can be challenging, especially as organizations scale their cloud infrastructure, deploy new applications, and manage dynamic workloads. SIEM solutions integrate with security orchestration, automation, and response (SOAR) platforms to automate segmentation policy adjustments based on detected security events. If SIEM detects an unauthorized access attempt or policy violation, it can automatically adjust firewall rules, restrict communication between segments, or quarantine suspicious workloads without manual intervention. This real-time enforcement ensures that segmentation policies remain effective against evolving threats.

Compliance monitoring is another critical aspect of SIEM in microsegmentation. Many industries, including finance, healthcare, and government, require organizations to enforce strict network segmentation policies to protect sensitive data and maintain regulatory compliance. Regulations such as PCI DSS, HIPAA, GDPR, and NIST mandate that organizations limit access to critical systems, monitor network activity, and maintain audit logs for security events. SIEM automates compliance reporting by continuously monitoring segmented environments, tracking access attempts, and generating audit-ready reports. This ensures that organizations can demonstrate compliance with regulatory requirements while maintaining robust security controls.

SIEM enhances visibility into microsegmented environments by providing security teams with a centralized dashboard that visualizes traffic flows, access patterns, and policy violations. Traditional network monitoring tools often struggle to provide deep visibility into highly segmented networks, where communication is restricted to predefined policies. SIEM overcomes this challenge by aggregating telemetry from multiple security sources, creating a unified view of network activity. Security analysts can drill down into specific segments, investigate suspicious behavior, and refine segmentation policies based on data-driven insights. This level of visibility helps organizations detect potential security gaps and continuously optimize their microsegmentation strategy.

Incident response is significantly improved through SIEM integration with microsegmentation. When a security incident occurs, organizations need to quickly identify the affected segment, isolate compromised systems, and prevent further damage. SIEM streamlines incident response by correlating security events, generating real-time alerts, and automating containment measures. For example, if SIEM detects an unauthorized attempt to access a restricted database, it can trigger an automated response to block the request, isolate the affected segment, and notify security teams. By integrating SIEM with microsegmentation, organizations can reduce incident response times and minimize the impact of security breaches.

Cloud environments pose unique challenges for SIEM-driven microsegmentation. Unlike traditional on-premises networks, cloud workloads are highly dynamic, frequently scaling up and down based on demand. SIEM solutions must integrate with cloud-native security tools, such as AWS GuardDuty, Azure Sentinel, and Google Security Command Center, to provide real-time monitoring and policy enforcement in cloud microsegmentation. By collecting cloud security logs, analyzing virtual network traffic, and correlating cloud-based security events, SIEM ensures that segmentation policies remain effective in hybrid and multi-cloud environments. This integration allows organizations to extend their microsegmentation strategy beyond on-premises data centers and into cloud infrastructures.

Encrypted traffic analysis is another area where SIEM enhances microsegmentation security. Many cyber threats use encryption to evade traditional security controls, making it difficult to inspect traffic between segmented workloads. SIEM solutions use advanced techniques such as machine learning, metadata analysis, and SSL/TLS decryption to identify suspicious activity within encrypted traffic. By monitoring communication patterns, identifying anomalies, and detecting hidden threats, SIEM helps organizations enforce segmentation policies even in environments where traffic is encrypted end-to-end. This ensures that security teams maintain visibility into potential threats without compromising data privacy.

The future of SIEM in microsegmentation will likely incorporate artificial intelligence, predictive analytics, and autonomous response mechanisms. AI-driven SIEM solutions will continuously refine segmentation policies based on real-time threat intelligence, automatically adjusting access controls to mitigate emerging risks. Predictive analytics will enable security teams to anticipate potential attack vectors and proactively enforce segmentation policies before threats materialize. Autonomous response mechanisms will allow SIEM to detect security incidents and dynamically reconfigure microsegmentation rules in real time, reducing the need for manual intervention and improving overall security resilience.

Organizations that integrate SIEM with microsegmentation gain enhanced security, improved threat detection, and faster incident response capabilities. By leveraging SIEM's real-time monitoring, behavioral analytics, and automation features, businesses can enforce adaptive segmentation policies that minimize attack surfaces and prevent unauthorized lateral movement. As cyber threats continue to evolve, the role of SIEM in microsegmentation will remain a critical component of modern security architectures, providing organizations with the visibility, intelligence, and automation needed to protect their digital assets.

Segmentation in Industrial Control Systems (ICS)

Segmentation in industrial control systems (ICS) is a critical security measure that protects critical infrastructure, manufacturing environments, and operational technology (OT) networks from cyber threats. Unlike traditional IT networks, ICS environments are designed to control physical processes, including power grids, water treatment plants, transportation systems, and industrial automation. These systems are essential for public safety, national security, and economic stability. However, the increasing connectivity of ICS to corporate networks, cloud services, and the internet has introduced new security risks. Segmentation plays a vital role in reducing the attack surface, limiting unauthorized access, and preventing cyber incidents from disrupting industrial operations.

Industrial control systems rely on specialized components such as programmable logic controllers (PLCs), supervisory control and data acquisition (SCADA) systems, human-machine interfaces (HMIs), and remote terminal units (RTUs). These components were traditionally designed with a focus on reliability and availability rather than security. Many legacy ICS devices lack built-in security controls, making them vulnerable to cyberattacks. Segmentation helps mitigate these risks by isolating critical control systems from IT networks, restricting communication between devices, and enforcing strict access policies. Without proper segmentation, a compromised IT system could provide attackers with a pathway to disrupt industrial operations.

A well-structured ICS segmentation strategy follows the Purdue Model for Industrial Control Systems, which defines different layers of network architecture to separate IT and OT environments. The Purdue Model consists of multiple levels, with enterprise systems at the top and industrial control devices at the lower levels. At the highest level, business and enterprise networks manage corporate operations, including data analytics, financial systems, and enterprise resource planning (ERP) applications. These networks should be strictly segmented from industrial control systems to prevent IT security incidents from impacting critical operations.

The next layer of the Purdue Model includes industrial demilitarized zones (IDMZs), which act as controlled security zones between IT and OT networks. IDMZs serve as a buffer that restricts direct communication between business systems and industrial networks. Firewalls, intrusion detection systems (IDS), and unidirectional security gateways enforce segmentation policies within the IDMZ, ensuring that only authorized traffic passes between the IT and OT environments. This segmentation strategy reduces the risk of malware infections, ransomware attacks, and unauthorized access to industrial control systems.

Further down the Purdue Model, segmentation is applied at the operational levels where SCADA systems, HMIs, and PLCs manage industrial processes. At this stage, microsegmentation enhances security by restricting communication between specific devices and control systems. Instead of allowing open communication across the entire industrial network, microsegmentation enforces granular access controls that limit interactions to only necessary connections. For example, a PLC responsible for controlling a manufacturing process should only communicate with its designated SCADA system, not with unrelated devices on the network. This prevents attackers from using lateral movement techniques to gain access to critical control functions.

Zero Trust principles further strengthen ICS segmentation by requiring continuous verification of devices, users, and network traffic. In traditional ICS environments, devices often operate with implicit trust, assuming that any system within the network is legitimate. However, this trust model is outdated and exposes industrial networks to insider threats and advanced persistent threats (APTs). By implementing Zero Trust segmentation, ICS networks enforce strict authentication, authorization, and monitoring for all communication between devices. Role-based access controls (RBAC) ensure that only authorized personnel and systems can access industrial processes, reducing the risk of unauthorized changes to critical systems.

Legacy ICS devices present additional challenges for segmentation because they were not designed with modern cybersecurity requirements in mind. Many industrial systems use outdated operating systems, proprietary communication protocols, and hardcoded credentials, making them difficult to secure. Segmentation strategies for legacy ICS environments often include virtual LANs (VLANs), firewalls, and air-gapped networks to limit exposure to external threats. In cases where full segmentation is not feasible, compensating security controls such as network monitoring, intrusion prevention systems (IPS), and secure remote access solutions provide additional protection.

114

Remote access to industrial control systems must be carefully segmented to prevent unauthorized users from gaining control over critical infrastructure. Many ICS environments require remote access for maintenance, monitoring, and troubleshooting by engineers and third-party vendors. However, insecure remote access solutions can become entry points for cyberattacks. Secure segmentation policies enforce multi-factor authentication (MFA), encrypted communication, and role-based access restrictions for remote connections. Virtual private networks (VPNs) and industrial-specific secure remote access solutions further enhance segmentation by ensuring that remote users only have access to designated systems.

Regulatory compliance plays a significant role in ICS segmentation strategies, as many industrial sectors are subject to strict cybersecurity regulations. Organizations operating critical infrastructure must comply with standards such as the NIST Cybersecurity Framework, IEC 62443, and the North American Electric Reliability Corporation Critical Infrastructure Protection (NERC CIP). These regulations require organizations to implement network segmentation, restrict access to control systems, and maintain audit logs for security events. SIEM solutions and security monitoring platforms integrate with segmentation policies to provide real-time visibility into network activity, ensuring compliance with regulatory requirements.

Monitoring and incident response are essential components of effective ICS segmentation. Security teams must continuously monitor segmented industrial networks to detect suspicious activity, unauthorized access attempts, and potential security breaches. Network security tools such as intrusion detection and prevention systems (IDPS), SIEM platforms, and anomaly detection solutions provide real-time insights into segmentation effectiveness. If an incident occurs, segmentation policies enable rapid response by isolating compromised segments, preventing attackers from spreading across the industrial network. Automated security playbooks and incident response plans further enhance segmentation by streamlining containment and recovery efforts.

The adoption of industrial IoT (IIoT) devices introduces new segmentation challenges in ICS environments. IIoT devices, including smart sensors, industrial robots, and connected monitoring systems, generate vast amounts of real-time data and often require internet connectivity. Without proper segmentation, IIoT devices can become attack vectors, exposing industrial networks to cyber threats. Segmentation strategies for IIoT include network zoning, software-defined segmentation, and strict access controls to ensure that IIoT devices only communicate with authorized control systems. Implementing security gateways and microsegmentation for IIoT further reduces the risk of unauthorized access and data breaches.

As cyber threats targeting ICS environments continue to evolve, segmentation remains a foundational security measure for protecting critical infrastructure. Organizations that implement robust segmentation strategies benefit from improved security, reduced attack surfaces, and increased resilience against cyberattacks. By leveraging best practices such as the Purdue Model, Zero Trust principles, and microsegmentation, ICS operators can ensure that industrial networks remain secure, reliable, and compliant with regulatory standards. The integration of segmentation with advanced security monitoring, incident response, and threat intelligence further enhances industrial cybersecurity, safeguarding essential operations from emerging cyber threats.

Microsegmentation for IoT Security

Microsegmentation for IoT security is a critical strategy for protecting connected devices from cyber threats, unauthorized access, and network-based attacks. As the number of Internet of Things (IoT) devices continues to grow across industries, organizations face increasing challenges in securing these devices, which often lack built-in security controls. IoT devices range from smart home appliances and industrial sensors to medical devices and critical infrastructure components, all of which generate vast amounts of data and require network connectivity. Without proper segmentation, these devices can become entry points for attackers, enabling lateral movement and potential compromise of critical systems. Microsegmentation provides a security solution by isolating IoT devices, enforcing strict communication policies, and reducing the attack surface within an organization's network.

Traditional network security models rely on perimeter-based defenses such as firewalls and intrusion prevention systems. However, IoT environments introduce new security risks because devices are often deployed in distributed locations, operate on proprietary firmware, and lack the capability to support traditional endpoint security software. Microsegmentation addresses these challenges by creating isolated network zones that restrict IoT devices from communicating with unauthorized systems. By applying fine-grained access controls, microsegmentation ensures that each IoT device only communicates with designated services, reducing the risk of unauthorized access and minimizing potential damage from a compromised device.

A major advantage of microsegmentation for IoT security is its ability to enforce least-privilege access. Unlike traditional segmentation methods that may allow broad access within a network segment, microsegmentation restricts communication between devices, ensuring that only necessary interactions occur. For example, a security camera should only communicate with the video management system and not with other networked devices such as workstations or enterprise servers. By implementing strict access policies, microsegmentation limits the spread of malware and prevents attackers from using compromised IoT devices to gain access to sensitive data or critical infrastructure.

IoT security is particularly challenging due to the diversity of devices, manufacturers, and communication protocols. Many IoT devices use proprietary or legacy protocols that do not support modern encryption and authentication mechanisms. Microsegmentation enables organizations to define security policies based on device identity, behavior, and traffic patterns rather than relying solely on IP addresses or traditional network zoning. Identity-based microsegmentation ensures that policies are dynamically applied based on device type, function, and risk level, allowing organizations to enforce adaptive security controls even in complex IoT environments.

Network visibility plays a crucial role in implementing effective microsegmentation for IoT security. Many organizations lack full visibility into the devices connected to their networks, making it difficult to enforce segmentation policies effectively. IoT security platforms integrate with microsegmentation solutions to provide real-time asset discovery, identifying all connected devices and their communication patterns. By continuously monitoring network traffic, security teams can detect unauthorized devices, analyze abnormal behavior, and refine segmentation policies to prevent security breaches. Enhanced visibility ensures that microsegmentation is applied correctly, minimizing blind spots that attackers could exploit.

Behavioral analytics strengthens microsegmentation by identifying deviations from normal IoT device activity. Machine learning and artificial intelligence analyze IoT traffic patterns to establish baselines for expected behavior, detecting anomalies that may indicate security threats. If an IoT device begins communicating with an unauthorized system or exhibits unusual traffic patterns, microsegmentation policies can automatically isolate the device, preventing potential attacks. This proactive approach enhances IoT security by detecting and responding to threats in real time, reducing the risk of data exfiltration or device manipulation.

IoT devices often require remote access for maintenance, updates, and troubleshooting. However, insecure remote access solutions can expose IoT networks to cyber threats. Microsegmentation enforces secure remote access by restricting maintenance sessions to authorized personnel and approved management tools. Instead of allowing direct access to IoT devices from the internet or untrusted networks, microsegmentation ensures that remote sessions pass through secure gateways with strict authentication and encryption protocols. By controlling how IoT devices are accessed and updated, microsegmentation reduces the risk of unauthorized modifications, firmware exploits, and insider threats.

Cloud integration further complicates IoT security, as many IoT devices rely on cloud-based management platforms for data processing, storage, and analytics. Organizations must ensure that cloud-connected IoT devices adhere to strict security policies that prevent unauthorized data transfers or cloud misconfigurations. Microsegmentation extends security controls to cloud environments by enforcing policies that restrict device communication based on workload identity, geolocation, and compliance requirements. By segmenting IoT devices that communicate with cloud services, organizations prevent data leaks and unauthorized access while maintaining regulatory compliance.

Regulatory requirements drive the adoption of microsegmentation for IoT security across various industries. Healthcare, finance, manufacturing, and critical infrastructure sectors must comply with regulations such as HIPAA, PCI DSS, and NIST cybersecurity frameworks, which mandate strict access controls and network segmentation. Microsegmentation helps organizations meet compliance requirements by enforcing least-privilege access, monitoring device activity, and generating audit logs for security incidents. Automated compliance enforcement ensures that IoT security policies remain aligned with regulatory standards, reducing the risk of non-compliance penalties and data breaches.

Incident response and threat containment benefit significantly from microsegmentation in IoT environments. When an IoT device is compromised, traditional security models may struggle to contain the threat due to the lack of granular access controls. Microsegmentation allows security teams to isolate compromised devices in real time, preventing lateral movement and reducing the impact of security incidents. Automated security playbooks and orchestration tools further enhance incident response by enforcing microsegmentation policies dynamically, ensuring that threats are contained before they spread across the network.

Challenges in implementing microsegmentation for IoT security include scalability, device diversity, and integration with legacy systems. Organizations managing thousands or millions of IoT devices must deploy segmentation strategies that scale efficiently while maintaining security effectiveness. Software-defined networking (SDN) and zero-trust network architectures support scalable microsegmentation by enabling centralized policy enforcement and dynamic access controls. Additionally, integration with existing security frameworks ensures that microsegmentation complements other IoT security measures, such as endpoint detection and response (EDR), intrusion detection systems (IDS), and security information and event management (SIEM) platforms.

Future advancements in microsegmentation for IoT security will leverage artificial intelligence, blockchain technology, and next-generation encryption to enhance device authentication, network isolation, and secure data exchange. AI-driven microsegmentation will enable automated threat detection and adaptive policy enforcement, while blockchain-based identity management will provide tamper-proof authentication for IoT devices. Enhanced encryption protocols will further secure IoT communications, preventing attackers from intercepting or manipulating sensitive data. As IoT ecosystems continue to expand, microsegmentation will remain a foundational security strategy for mitigating cyber risks and protecting connected devices.

Organizations that implement microsegmentation for IoT security benefit from reduced attack surfaces, improved compliance, and stronger network defenses. By enforcing identity-based policies, leveraging behavioral analytics, and securing remote access, businesses can protect IoT devices from evolving cyber threats. As IoT adoption increases across industries, microsegmentation will play a crucial role in securing critical infrastructure, preventing unauthorized access, and ensuring the integrity of connected ecosystems. With continuous advancements in security technologies, microsegmentation will remain a cornerstone of IoT security, enabling organizations to mitigate risks while maximizing the benefits of connected devices.

Compliance and Regulatory Requirements

Compliance and regulatory requirements play a fundamental role in shaping cybersecurity strategies, particularly in the implementation of network segmentation and microsegmentation. As organizations operate in increasingly complex digital environments, regulatory frameworks establish guidelines for protecting sensitive data, preventing unauthorized access, and mitigating security risks. Compliance is not only a legal obligation but also a critical component of a robust cybersecurity posture. Organizations that fail to meet regulatory standards risk legal penalties, reputational damage, and increased exposure to cyber threats. By adhering to compliance requirements and implementing effective segmentation strategies, businesses can enhance security, reduce attack surfaces, and ensure that sensitive information remains protected.

Various regulatory bodies and industry-specific standards mandate the implementation of network segmentation as a fundamental security control. Regulations such as the General Data Protection Regulation (GDPR), the Health Insurance Portability and Accountability Act (HIPAA), the Payment Card Industry Data Security Standard (PCI DSS), and the National Institute of Standards and Technology (NIST) Cybersecurity Framework all emphasize the importance of access control and data protection. These regulations require organizations to limit access to sensitive data, restrict network communications based on security policies, and continuously monitor for potential security incidents. Network segmentation and microsegmentation enable organizations to meet these requirements by enforcing least-privilege access, isolating critical systems, and preventing unauthorized movement within the network.

GDPR, a global privacy regulation enacted by the European Union, imposes strict requirements on organizations that process personal data. One of its key provisions is the principle of data minimization, which mandates that organizations should collect and process only the data necessary for legitimate purposes. Network segmentation supports GDPR compliance by restricting access to personal data based on user roles and responsibilities. By implementing segmentation policies, organizations ensure that only authorized personnel can access sensitive information, reducing the risk of unauthorized exposure. Additionally, GDPR requires organizations to implement security measures that prevent data breaches. Microsegmentation enhances security by containing potential breaches and preventing attackers from moving laterally within the network, reducing the risk of widespread data exposure.

HIPAA, which governs the protection of patient health information (PHI) in the United States, mandates strict security controls for healthcare organizations. One of the key provisions of HIPAA is the requirement to implement access controls that limit access to PHI based on job function and necessity. Network segmentation is an effective way to enforce this requirement by separating PHI storage and processing systems from general IT infrastructure. Hospitals, clinics, and healthcare providers use segmentation to isolate electronic health records, medical devices, and administrative systems, preventing unauthorized access to sensitive patient data. Microsegmentation further strengthens HIPAA compliance by enforcing granular access controls at the workload level, ensuring that only authorized applications and users can interact with PHI.

PCI DSS, which applies to organizations handling credit card transactions, requires strict network segmentation to protect cardholder data. One of the primary security requirements of PCI DSS is the isolation of the Cardholder Data Environment (CDE) from the rest of the network. Organizations must implement firewalls, access control mechanisms, and network segmentation policies to ensure that only authorized systems can access payment processing environments. Microsegmentation provides an additional layer of security by enforcing transaction-specific access controls, preventing unauthorized communication between payment processing systems and other network segments. By limiting exposure to cardholder data and restricting lateral movement, organizations can reduce the risk of payment fraud and comply with PCI DSS requirements.

The NIST Cybersecurity Framework provides a comprehensive set of security guidelines for organizations across various industries. One of its key principles is the implementation of layered security controls to mitigate cyber risks. Network segmentation aligns with NIST recommendations by creating multiple security zones that prevent attackers from accessing critical assets. The framework also emphasizes continuous monitoring, threat detection, and incident response as essential components of a cybersecurity strategy. SIEM and security analytics platforms integrate with segmentation policies to provide real-time visibility into network activity, ensuring that organizations can detect and respond to security incidents in accordance with NIST guidelines.

Regulatory compliance also plays a crucial role in securing industrial control systems (ICS) and critical infrastructure. The North American Electric Reliability Corporation Critical Infrastructure Protection (NERC CIP) standards mandate strict access controls and segmentation measures for power grid operators and energy providers. ICS environments are particularly vulnerable to cyber threats due to their reliance on legacy systems and real-time operational processes. Segmentation is essential for protecting ICS networks from cyberattacks by isolating control systems from corporate IT networks and external threats. Microsegmentation further enhances ICS security by enforcing workload-specific access controls, ensuring that only authorized devices and personnel can interact with industrial control systems.

Financial institutions must comply with regulations such as the Sarbanes-Oxley Act (SOX) and the Federal Financial Institutions Examination Council (FFIEC) guidelines, which require organizations to implement security measures that protect financial data and customer transactions. Network segmentation is a key component of financial sector security, ensuring that sensitive banking applications, transaction processing systems, and customer records are isolated from external threats. By implementing microsegmentation, financial organizations can enforce strict access controls, prevent unauthorized communication between financial applications, and enhance fraud detection capabilities. Compliance with these regulations helps financial institutions protect sensitive financial data while maintaining the integrity of banking operations.

Cloud security compliance is another critical consideration for organizations operating in hybrid and multi-cloud environments. Regulations such as the Federal Risk and Authorization Management Program (FedRAMP) and the Cloud Security Alliance (CSA) Cloud Controls Matrix provide security guidelines for organizations using cloud services. Cloud environments introduce unique challenges due to their dynamic nature, making segmentation an essential security measure. Organizations must implement cloud-native segmentation policies that restrict data access, enforce identity-based security controls, and monitor network activity in real time. Microsegmentation extends security to cloud workloads by preventing unauthorized interactions between cloud-based applications, ensuring compliance with cloud security standards.

Automated compliance enforcement is essential for maintaining regulatory adherence in dynamic IT environments. Traditional compliance management processes rely on manual audits, which can be time-consuming and prone to human error. Organizations can enhance compliance efforts by integrating segmentation policies with automated security controls, allowing real-time enforcement of regulatory requirements. Security orchestration platforms provide automated compliance monitoring, generating reports, detecting policy violations, and ensuring that segmentation policies remain aligned with industry regulations. By leveraging automation, organizations can streamline compliance efforts, reduce administrative overhead, and ensure continuous regulatory adherence.

Maintaining compliance with regulatory requirements is an ongoing process that requires continuous monitoring, policy adjustments, and security enhancements. Cyber threats are constantly evolving, and regulatory frameworks frequently update their security requirements to address emerging risks. Organizations must remain proactive in updating segmentation policies, conducting security assessments, and implementing new security measures to meet compliance standards. By integrating segmentation with security monitoring, threat intelligence, and incident response capabilities, organizations can ensure that their networks remain secure, resilient, and compliant with industry regulations.

By adhering to compliance and regulatory requirements, organizations enhance their cybersecurity posture, protect sensitive data, and reduce the risk of security breaches. Network segmentation and microsegmentation serve as foundational security measures that align with regulatory mandates, enforce least-privilege access, and prevent unauthorized movement within networks. As cyber threats continue to evolve, regulatory compliance will remain a driving force in shaping security strategies, ensuring that organizations implement the necessary controls to safeguard their digital assets and maintain trust with customers, stakeholders, and regulatory authorities.

Case Studies: Successful Network Segmentation Implementations

Network segmentation has proven to be a fundamental cybersecurity measure in preventing breaches, limiting lateral movement, and securing sensitive data across various industries. Organizations across finance, healthcare, manufacturing, and critical infrastructure have successfully implemented segmentation strategies to enhance security, comply with regulations, and improve operational efficiency. By studying real-world implementations, businesses can understand how segmentation can be applied effectively, the challenges involved, and the benefits that follow. The following case studies highlight successful network segmentation projects that have strengthened security postures and mitigated cyber threats.

A large financial institution faced increasing cybersecurity threats, including phishing attacks and insider threats that could potentially expose customer financial data. The institution had a flat network architecture that allowed excessive internal communication, making it vulnerable to lateral movement if an attacker compromised a single endpoint. To address this, the organization implemented a microsegmentation strategy using a software-defined networking (SDN) approach. Segmentation policies were based on identity, application behavior, and contextual risk factors rather than relying solely on IP-based controls. Customer transaction systems were isolated from internal IT systems, employee workstations were restricted from communicating with high-value assets, and third-party vendors were provided with limited, controlled access. The implementation significantly reduced the risk of unauthorized access and potential data breaches. By integrating microsegmentation with Security Information and Event Management (SIEM) systems, the institution gained real-time visibility into segmentation policy violations and anomalous traffic patterns, enabling faster incident response. The successful deployment of network segmentation not only enhanced security but also ensured compliance with PCI DSS and other financial regulations.

A leading hospital network experienced a ransomware attack that encrypted patient records and disrupted critical medical services. The attack spread quickly due to a lack of network segmentation between medical devices, administrative systems, and research databases. After recovering from the incident, the hospital implemented a robust network segmentation framework to prevent future attacks. Medical devices such as MRI machines, infusion pumps, and monitoring systems were placed in isolated network segments, ensuring they could only communicate with authorized hospital servers and not with general IT workstations or internet-connected devices. Patient records were stored in a secured, segmented environment with strict access controls, preventing unauthorized access from compromised endpoints. Remote access for third-party vendors responsible for medical equipment maintenance was restricted through a Zero Trust model, requiring multi-factor authentication and session monitoring. The hospital also implemented continuous traffic analysis to detect unusual communication patterns and potential lateral movement attempts. Following the segmentation project, the hospital strengthened its resilience against ransomware and improved compliance with HIPAA regulations.

A global manufacturing company faced challenges in securing its operational technology (OT) environment, which included industrial control systems (ICS), programmable logic controllers (PLCs), and robotic automation systems. The company was expanding its digital transformation efforts, integrating Industrial IoT (IIoT) devices to improve efficiency. However, this increased the attack surface, exposing OT networks to potential cyber threats originating from IT systems. The company implemented a segmentation strategy based on the Purdue Model for ICS security. The corporate IT network was completely separated from the OT network through an industrial demilitarized zone (IDMZ), preventing direct communication between business applications and critical manufacturing processes. Within the OT network, microsegmentation policies were applied to isolate different production lines, ensuring that a compromise in one system would not affect others. Role-based access control (RBAC) was enforced to limit access to sensitive manufacturing systems, and anomaly detection tools were integrated to monitor for potential attacks against ICS components. The segmentation project not only enhanced security but also ensured compliance with industrial cybersecurity standards such as IEC 62443 and NIST 800-82.

A multinational retailer with thousands of stores and distribution centers worldwide struggled with securing its point-of-sale (POS) systems from cyberattacks. The company's previous network architecture allowed store devices, employee workstations, and payment terminals to communicate freely, increasing the risk of data breaches and credit card fraud. To address this, the retailer implemented a network segmentation framework that isolated POS systems from all other network segments. Each store was assigned a dedicated, segmented network for payment processing, preventing potential attackers from accessing payment terminals even if they breached another system within the store. Employee devices and in-store guest Wi-Fi were placed in separate network segments with strictly enforced access controls. The segmentation project was integrated with cloud security policies to ensure that remote monitoring and transaction processing remained secure. The retailer also leveraged SIEM and machine learning-based analytics to monitor for suspicious activity, providing early detection of potential fraud attempts. This segmentation strategy significantly reduced the risk of credit card data theft and ensured compliance with PCI DSS requirements.

A national energy provider responsible for managing power grids and critical infrastructure faced persistent cyber threats, including attempts to breach its industrial control systems. The company relied on legacy network architectures that provided minimal segmentation between IT and OT environments. This lack of segmentation created a high-risk scenario where a breach in the corporate IT network could allow attackers to access critical infrastructure controls. The energy provider initiated a segmentation project that involved deploying next-generation firewalls, air-gapped network zones, and microsegmentation within its OT environment. All ICS components were isolated from the internet, and real-time monitoring was implemented to detect unauthorized communication attempts. Secure remote access was enforced for field technicians, requiring authentication through a segmented gateway that restricted access based on job function. The segmentation framework complied with NERC CIP regulations and improved the provider's overall security resilience, reducing the risk of cyber threats impacting national energy infrastructure.

A technology company specializing in cloud-based applications faced increasing concerns about insider threats and data exfiltration. With a large remote workforce and multiple cloud deployments, enforcing security controls across hybrid environments was a challenge. The company adopted an identity-based microsegmentation strategy that controlled access to applications and services based on user identity and device posture. Multi-cloud security policies were applied to enforce segmentation rules across AWS, Azure, and Google Cloud environments, ensuring that workloads remained isolated and could only communicate based on predefined policies. The company implemented behavioral analytics to detect anomalies, such as unauthorized data transfers or excessive privilege escalations. Automated enforcement of segmentation policies prevented unauthorized access to sensitive intellectual property, reducing insider threat risks while maintaining a seamless user experience. The successful deployment of microsegmentation allowed the company to enhance security without disrupting business operations, ensuring compliance with data protection regulations such as GDPR.

Each of these case studies demonstrates the effectiveness of network segmentation in mitigating cyber risks, improving compliance, and ensuring business continuity. Whether applied in financial institutions, healthcare organizations, manufacturing environments, retail businesses, or critical infrastructure, segmentation provides a proactive defense against modern cyber threats. By implementing segmentation strategies tailored to their specific needs, organizations can create secure network architectures that prevent lateral movement, limit exposure to attacks, and safeguard sensitive data.

Common Pitfalls in Segmentation Strategies

Implementing network segmentation is a critical security measure that strengthens access control, reduces the attack surface, and limits lateral movement within an organization's infrastructure. However, segmentation strategies can fail if they are not properly planned, implemented, or maintained. Many organizations fall into common pitfalls that weaken security, introduce operational inefficiencies, and create unintended vulnerabilities. Understanding these challenges can help organizations refine their segmentation approach, avoid costly mistakes, and ensure that segmentation policies provide the intended level of security and functionality.

One of the most common pitfalls in segmentation strategies is over-segmentation. Organizations attempting to enforce strict security controls may create too many segments, leading to excessive complexity in network management. Over-segmentation can result in unnecessary administrative overhead, increased latency, and performance issues as traffic must pass through multiple security layers. Security teams may struggle to manage and update access policies, leading to operational inefficiencies and potential misconfigurations. Users and applications may also experience disruptions if segmentation policies are too restrictive, causing legitimate traffic to be blocked and reducing overall productivity. Effective segmentation should balance security with usability, ensuring that policies are granular enough to enforce security controls without negatively impacting network performance.

Conversely, under-segmentation is another major pitfall where organizations fail to create sufficient security boundaries. Many networks still operate with a flat architecture where devices, applications, and users can communicate freely without restrictions. This lack of segmentation increases the risk of lateral movement in the event of a security breach. If an attacker gains access to an endpoint in an under-segmented network, they can move undetected to more critical assets, such as databases, servers, or cloud environments. Organizations that do not implement proper segmentation expose themselves to ransomware attacks, insider threats, and data breaches. Security teams should ensure that segmentation strategies establish clear boundaries between critical assets while maintaining necessary functionality.

A lack of visibility into network traffic and asset inventory is another challenge that can lead to ineffective segmentation. Many organizations deploy segmentation policies without a complete understanding of how different systems interact or what communication flows are necessary for business operations. Without proper traffic analysis, security teams may misconfigure policies that block essential connections or fail to restrict unauthorized access. A lack of visibility also makes it difficult to detect segmentation policy violations or unauthorized access attempts. Organizations must use network monitoring tools, Security Information and Event Management (SIEM) platforms, and behavioral analytics to gain insight into network activity and ensure that segmentation policies align with actual traffic flows.

Poorly defined segmentation policies can create security gaps that attackers can exploit. If segmentation rules are not properly configured, malicious actors may find unintended pathways to critical assets. Common mistakes include allowing excessive exceptions to access rules, failing to apply consistent policies across different network environments, and not regularly reviewing segmentation policies for outdated rules. Organizations should implement a standardized approach to segmentation policy design, ensuring that access controls follow the principle of least privilege. Policies should be regularly audited and updated to reflect changes in network architecture, user roles, and business requirements.

Failure to integrate segmentation with identity and access management (IAM) is another common mistake that weakens security. Traditional segmentation approaches rely on static rules, such as IP-based access controls, which do not account for user identities or contextual risk factors. Modern segmentation strategies should incorporate identity-based access controls that enforce policies based on user authentication, device posture, and real-time security assessments. By integrating segmentation with IAM solutions, organizations can ensure that access to critical resources is dynamically controlled based on user roles, behavioral analytics, and risk levels.

Inconsistent segmentation policies across hybrid and multi-cloud environments can create security gaps and operational challenges. Many organizations operate in hybrid environments where workloads are distributed between on-premises data centers and multiple cloud providers. If segmentation policies are not consistently applied across all environments, attackers may exploit misconfigurations to gain unauthorized access. Cloud environments introduce additional complexities, such as ephemeral workloads, containerized applications, and identity-based security models, which require specialized segmentation strategies. Organizations should adopt cloud-native security tools, automated policy enforcement mechanisms, and centralized management platforms to ensure uniform segmentation policies across hybrid and multi-cloud architectures.

A failure to account for encrypted traffic can also compromise segmentation effectiveness. Many modern applications and cloud services use end-to-end encryption to protect data in transit. While encryption enhances data security, it also makes it more difficult for security tools to inspect traffic and enforce segmentation policies. Attackers may use encrypted channels to bypass traditional security controls, enabling them to move undetected within a segmented network. Organizations must implement encrypted traffic analysis solutions, such as SSL/TLS decryption, machine learning-based anomaly detection, and metadata inspection, to maintain visibility into network activity while preserving data privacy.

Lack of automation and orchestration in segmentation management can lead to misconfigurations, delays in policy updates, and increased administrative overhead. Manually managing segmentation policies across large-scale environments is time-consuming and prone to human error. Security teams may struggle to keep up with changes in network architecture, application deployments, and user access requirements. Automation solutions, such as infrastructure-as-code (IaC), security orchestration platforms, and AI-driven policy management tools, enable organizations to dynamically enforce segmentation rules based on real-time traffic analysis, security alerts, and compliance requirements. Automating segmentation policies improves efficiency, reduces human error, and enhances overall security posture.

Neglecting compliance requirements when designing segmentation strategies can lead to regulatory violations and financial penalties. Many industries, including finance, healthcare, and critical infrastructure, are subject to strict data protection regulations that mandate network segmentation as a security control. Failure to implement compliant segmentation policies may result in data breaches, loss of customer trust, and legal consequences. Organizations should align segmentation strategies with regulatory frameworks such as GDPR, HIPAA, PCI DSS, and NIST guidelines. Compliance monitoring tools can automate policy enforcement, generate audit logs, and provide real-time insights into regulatory compliance status.

Inadequate testing and validation of segmentation policies can lead to security gaps that remain undetected until a breach occurs. Many organizations deploy segmentation strategies without thoroughly testing their effectiveness under real-world conditions. Misconfigurations, overlooked access rules, or unexpected traffic patterns may compromise segmentation security. Regular penetration testing, red teaming exercises, and segmentation audits help identify weaknesses and ensure that policies function as intended. Security teams should also simulate attack scenarios to evaluate how well segmentation controls prevent lateral movement and contain threats.

Failure to educate employees and stakeholders about segmentation policies can create security vulnerabilities due to human error. Many security incidents occur because users unknowingly bypass segmentation controls, use unauthorized communication channels, or fail to follow security best practices. Organizations should provide training and awareness programs to ensure that employees, IT administrators, and third-party vendors understand segmentation policies and their role in maintaining network security. Clear communication of access controls, policy enforcement mechanisms, and acceptable use guidelines helps reduce the risk of accidental policy violations.

Avoiding these common pitfalls in segmentation strategies requires a proactive approach that balances security, functionality, and operational efficiency. Organizations must continuously refine their segmentation policies, leverage automation, maintain visibility into network activity, and integrate identity-based controls to create a robust segmentation framework. By addressing these challenges, organizations can enhance their overall security posture, reduce attack surfaces, and prevent unauthorized access to critical assets.

Testing and Validating Segmentation Policies

Testing and validating segmentation policies is a critical step in ensuring that network segmentation functions as intended, providing security, compliance, and operational efficiency. Without proper validation, segmentation policies may contain misconfigurations, excessive access permissions, or gaps that attackers can exploit. Organizations that implement segmentation must establish a systematic approach to testing and validation to confirm that policies effectively limit access, enforce least-privilege principles, and prevent unauthorized lateral movement. Continuous validation is essential in dynamic environments where networks evolve, applications are updated, and security threats constantly change.

One of the key objectives of testing segmentation policies is to verify that access controls enforce the intended security boundaries. Segmentation policies should be designed to separate sensitive assets from general network traffic while allowing legitimate communication between authorized systems. Testing ensures that segmentation rules do not unintentionally block necessary traffic, which could disrupt business operations, or allow excessive permissions that could expose critical resources. Organizations must conduct access control tests to confirm that only approved users, devices, and applications can communicate across segmented boundaries. Security teams should use predefined scenarios that mimic real-world access requests to validate whether segmentation rules function as expected.

Penetration testing is an essential method for evaluating segmentation policies. Ethical hackers and red teams simulate cyberattacks to identify weaknesses in segmentation controls. These tests attempt to bypass access restrictions, escalate privileges, and move laterally within the network. If penetration testers successfully access restricted segments, it indicates that segmentation policies require refinement. Red team exercises simulate attacker behavior, testing whether segmentation prevents unauthorized access to sensitive data, cloud workloads, or industrial control systems. The results of penetration testing provide valuable insights into potential misconfigurations, policy gaps, and areas where segmentation rules need to be strengthened.

Network traffic analysis plays a vital role in segmentation validation. Organizations must continuously monitor traffic flows to detect unauthorized communications between network segments. If a segmentation policy is not enforced correctly, unexpected traffic patterns may indicate that an improperly configured rule is allowing unauthorized connections. Security teams should use tools such as Security Information and Event Management (SIEM), flow analytics, and packet inspection to analyze traffic and validate segmentation effectiveness. By examining network telemetry, security teams can detect policy violations, anomalous traffic, and segmentation rule misconfigurations before they become security risks.

Firewalls and intrusion detection/prevention systems (IDS/IPS) must be tested to ensure that segmentation policies correctly enforce access controls. Firewall rule validation ensures that only necessary ports and protocols are open within each network segment. Misconfigured firewall rules can create security gaps that allow attackers to bypass segmentation controls. Security teams should conduct firewall audits to confirm that segmentation rules align with security policies, blocking unauthorized traffic while allowing necessary business operations. IDS/IPS solutions should also be tested to verify that they detect and alert security teams to segmentation policy violations, suspicious traffic, or attempted lateral movement.

Zero Trust segmentation requires continuous validation through automated security assessments. Zero Trust architectures enforce strict access controls based on identity, device health, and real-time risk analysis. Organizations using Zero Trust segmentation must validate that access requests are dynamically evaluated and that unauthorized users cannot bypass security controls. Automated security validation tools simulate access attempts under different conditions to test whether Zero Trust policies are applied consistently. These tools analyze authentication processes, session monitoring, and access enforcement to ensure that segmentation policies adapt to risk-based security conditions.

Compliance validation is another critical component of segmentation testing. Many industries, including finance, healthcare, and government, have regulatory requirements that mandate network segmentation to protect sensitive data. Organizations must conduct compliance audits to verify that segmentation policies align with regulations such as GDPR, HIPAA, PCI DSS, and NIST frameworks. Compliance testing ensures that segmentation effectively isolates regulated data, enforces encryption standards, and maintains audit logs for security reviews. Organizations should use compliance assessment tools to generate reports, track policy adherence, and identify areas where segmentation policies need adjustments to meet regulatory requirements.

Segmentation policy validation should include stress testing to evaluate how the network performs under heavy traffic loads. Some segmentation implementations may introduce latency or performance bottlenecks if policies are not optimized. Security teams must conduct stress tests to measure how segmentation policies impact network speed, application availability, and overall system performance. Load testing tools simulate high volumes of network traffic to determine whether segmentation policies cause delays or disruptions. If performance issues arise, segmentation rules may need to be refined to balance security with efficiency.

Organizations should also conduct segmentation validation through scenario-based testing. Security teams can create hypothetical attack scenarios to test how segmentation policies respond to different threats. These scenarios may include attempts to access critical databases, exploit misconfigured firewall rules, or move laterally across cloud environments. By simulating real-world attacks, organizations can identify potential weaknesses in segmentation policies and refine their security posture. Scenario-based testing provides insights into whether segmentation rules effectively contain threats and whether security teams can detect and respond to segmentation violations in a timely manner.

Change management plays a crucial role in segmentation validation. As networks evolve, new applications, devices, and users may require changes to segmentation policies. Organizations must implement change management procedures to ensure that segmentation rules remain effective as IT environments change. Security teams should validate segmentation policies after every significant network change, application deployment, or infrastructure upgrade. Automated policy verification tools can help ensure that changes do not introduce security gaps or disrupt existing segmentation controls. Regular policy reviews help organizations maintain a secure segmentation framework while adapting to business needs.

Organizations should leverage automation to streamline segmentation validation processes. Manual testing is time-consuming and prone to human error, making it difficult to maintain effective segmentation policies at scale. Automated security validation platforms continuously assess segmentation effectiveness, analyze network traffic, and identify potential vulnerabilities. These platforms use AI-driven analytics to detect segmentation policy deviations, generate security alerts, and recommend corrective actions. Automation ensures that segmentation policies remain enforceable across hybrid and multi-cloud environments, reducing the risk of misconfigurations and security breaches.

Continuous validation is essential to maintaining segmentation security. Organizations cannot rely on a one-time segmentation deployment; they must conduct ongoing validation to ensure that policies remain effective against evolving cyber threats. Security teams should implement continuous monitoring, scheduled segmentation tests, and automated policy audits to identify weaknesses and proactively address security gaps. By integrating validation into routine security operations, organizations can maintain strong segmentation controls that adapt to new threats, regulatory changes, and technological advancements.

Organizations that implement rigorous segmentation testing and validation processes strengthen their cybersecurity posture, improve compliance, and enhance operational resilience. By proactively identifying and addressing segmentation weaknesses, businesses can ensure that network segmentation provides the intended level of security while maintaining efficiency and scalability. With a combination of penetration testing, network traffic analysis, compliance validation, and automation, organizations can build a robust segmentation framework that effectively protects their digital assets from modern cyber threats.

Incident Response and Segmented Networks

Incident response is a critical aspect of cybersecurity that ensures organizations can quickly detect, contain, and recover from security breaches. In highly segmented networks, incident response strategies must be carefully designed to take advantage of segmentation while addressing the complexities it introduces. Segmentation enhances security by limiting lateral movement and isolating critical assets, but it also adds operational challenges that must be managed during an incident. A well-planned incident response framework in a segmented network environment ensures that security teams can efficiently investigate threats, contain compromised segments, and restore normal operations without disrupting essential business functions.

One of the key benefits of segmented networks in incident response is the containment of threats. In a flat network, once an attacker gains access to an endpoint, they can move laterally to compromise other systems. In a segmented network, security teams can leverage segmentation policies to prevent unauthorized movement between network segments, minimizing the attack surface. If a ransomware attack compromises a workstation in one segment, proper segmentation ensures that it cannot spread to other critical systems such as financial databases, cloud workloads, or operational technology environments. Incident response teams must be trained to leverage segmentation controls effectively, using predefined isolation policies to contain threats quickly before they escalate.

Detection and monitoring are essential components of an incident response strategy in a segmented network. Security teams must have visibility into all network segments to detect suspicious activity and policy violations. Many organizations deploy Security Information and Event Management (SIEM) systems, network detection and response (NDR) tools, and endpoint detection and response (EDR) solutions to monitor segmentation policies in real time. These tools provide security analysts with insights into attempted lateral movement, unauthorized access attempts, and anomalous traffic patterns. By continuously analyzing network activity, organizations can detect potential incidents early and prevent attackers from navigating through segmented environments undetected.

Automated threat containment is a critical capability in segmented networks. When a security incident is detected, predefined automation policies should trigger an immediate response to isolate compromised assets. Security orchestration, automation, and response (SOAR) platforms can integrate with segmentation policies to automatically quarantine infected endpoints, block malicious network traffic, and disable compromised user accounts. By automating containment processes, organizations reduce response times and minimize the potential impact of a security incident. Incident response teams should regularly test automation workflows to ensure they function correctly and align with segmentation policies.

Incident response plans must account for access control restrictions introduced by network segmentation. In a highly segmented environment, security teams may face challenges accessing certain systems during an investigation. If access policies are too restrictive, incident responders may be unable to collect logs, analyze forensic data, or deploy remediation tools in real time. Organizations must establish emergency access protocols that allow security personnel to bypass segmentation controls in a controlled manner during an active investigation. These emergency access procedures should be carefully documented, require multi-factor authentication, and include detailed logging to ensure accountability.

Forensic analysis is a crucial step in incident response, and segmented networks require a tailored approach to forensic data collection. Since different network segments may have varying access restrictions, security teams must establish logging and telemetry collection mechanisms across all segments. Centralized logging solutions aggregate forensic data from various network segments, providing analysts with a comprehensive view of an incident. By analyzing log files, network traffic captures, and endpoint activity, investigators can determine the root cause of an incident, identify affected systems, and develop a remediation strategy. Effective forensic analysis helps organizations refine their segmentation policies to prevent similar incidents in the future.

Communication and coordination are vital during incident response in a segmented network. Security teams, IT personnel, and executive leadership must have a clear understanding of segmentation policies and how they impact response efforts. During a security event, cross-functional teams must collaborate to assess the scope of the incident, implement containment measures, and execute recovery procedures. Incident response plans should include predefined communication protocols to ensure that the right stakeholders receive timely and accurate information. Secure communication channels should be established to prevent attackers from intercepting response team discussions.

Testing and simulation exercises help organizations refine their incident response strategies in segmented networks. Conducting tabletop exercises, red team assessments, and penetration testing allows security teams to evaluate their ability to detect and respond to incidents within a segmented environment. These exercises simulate real-world attack scenarios, testing how well segmentation policies prevent unauthorized access and how efficiently response teams can contain threats. By analyzing the results of these simulations, organizations can identify weaknesses in their segmentation and incident response strategies and implement necessary improvements.

Cloud environments add complexity to incident response in segmented networks. Many organizations operate in multi-cloud or hybrid environments, requiring incident response teams to coordinate across different cloud providers, data centers, and on-premises infrastructures. Cloud-native segmentation tools, such as security groups, virtual private networks (VPNs), and identity-based access controls, must be integrated into the incident response framework. Security teams should have visibility into cloud traffic, log management systems, and threat intelligence platforms to detect and respond to security incidents affecting cloud workloads. Standardized response procedures should be in place to ensure that cloud-based segmentation policies align with on-premises security controls.

Regulatory compliance considerations must also be addressed in incident response strategies for segmented networks. Many industries require organizations to follow specific guidelines for responding to security incidents, reporting breaches, and maintaining forensic evidence. Regulations such as the General Data Protection Regulation (GDPR), the Health Insurance Portability and Accountability Act (HIPAA), and the Payment Card Industry Data Security Standard (PCI DSS) impose strict requirements for incident handling. Segmented networks must be designed to ensure that forensic data is retained for regulatory audits and that response teams can demonstrate compliance with incident management best practices.

Incident response strategies should include post-incident reviews to evaluate the effectiveness of segmentation policies. After an incident is contained and resolved, security teams must conduct a detailed review to identify lessons learned. These reviews should assess whether segmentation policies effectively prevented lateral movement, whether detection and response mechanisms functioned as expected, and whether automation tools successfully contained the threat. Organizations should use these findings to update segmentation rules, improve incident response playbooks, and enhance monitoring capabilities. Continuous improvement ensures that segmented networks remain resilient against future threats.

Organizations that integrate network segmentation with incident response benefit from stronger security, reduced risk exposure, and improved resilience against cyberattacks. By leveraging segmentation for threat containment, implementing automated response mechanisms, and refining forensic analysis processes, businesses can minimize the impact of security incidents. Security teams must continuously test and refine incident response plans to account for the complexities of segmented environments, ensuring that threats are detected and neutralized before they escalate. By aligning segmentation strategies with incident response best practices, organizations can enhance their overall cybersecurity posture and maintain business continuity in the face of evolving threats.

Risk Management and Network Segmentation

Risk management is a fundamental aspect of cybersecurity, ensuring that organizations can identify, assess, and mitigate threats to their digital infrastructure. Network segmentation plays a crucial role in risk management by reducing the attack surface, limiting unauthorized access, and preventing lateral movement within an organization's network. A well-structured segmentation strategy helps security teams prioritize risks, enforce access controls, and align security measures with business objectives. By integrating network segmentation into a broader risk management framework, organizations can enhance resilience, maintain compliance, and minimize the impact of cyber threats.

One of the primary objectives of risk management is to identify and categorize risks based on their potential impact and likelihood. Not all assets within a network have the same level of sensitivity or exposure to threats. A flat network architecture, where all devices and applications can communicate without restrictions, increases the risk of widespread attacks. Network segmentation mitigates these risks by isolating critical assets, ensuring that even if a security incident occurs, its impact is limited to a specific segment. By conducting a risk assessment, organizations can determine which assets require the highest level of protection and apply segmentation policies accordingly.

Segmentation supports the principle of least privilege, a key concept in risk management that restricts access to only what is necessary for a user, device, or application. Without proper segmentation, employees, contractors, and third-party vendors may have access to systems that are not relevant to their roles, increasing the risk of insider threats or accidental data exposure. Role-based segmentation ensures that access permissions align with business requirements while reducing the risk of unauthorized actions. Risk assessments should evaluate user access patterns, identifying areas where segmentation can prevent excessive privileges from leading to security breaches.

Risk management frameworks such as NIST, ISO 27001, and CIS Controls emphasize the importance of network segmentation in protecting critical infrastructure and sensitive data. These frameworks guide organizations in implementing segmentation as part of a layered security approach, ensuring that risks are mitigated at multiple levels. Compliance with these frameworks helps organizations establish standardized risk management processes, reducing exposure to cyber threats while maintaining regulatory compliance. Regular risk assessments should evaluate segmentation effectiveness, ensuring that policies remain aligned with evolving security requirements and business objectives.

Threat modeling is an essential component of risk management that identifies potential attack vectors and determines how segmentation can prevent or mitigate them. Organizations must assess how attackers might attempt to compromise their networks, move laterally between systems, and exfiltrate sensitive data. Threat models should consider various attack scenarios, such as credential theft, phishing campaigns, and ransomware infections, to determine how segmentation can serve as a defense mechanism. By analyzing different attack paths, security teams can design segmentation policies that minimize risk and contain potential security incidents before they escalate.

Microsegmentation enhances risk management by applying granular access controls at the workload level. Traditional segmentation methods, such as VLANs and firewall rules, create broad network zones that may still allow lateral movement within segments. Microsegmentation refines this approach by restricting communication between individual applications, servers, and virtual machines based on predefined security policies. This ensures that even if an attacker compromises one system, they cannot easily access other systems within the same segment. Risk assessments should evaluate the need for microsegmentation in environments that handle sensitive data, process financial transactions, or support critical business functions.

Network segmentation also plays a critical role in mitigating supply chain risks. Many organizations rely on third-party vendors, cloud service providers, and external contractors, introducing additional security risks. A compromised vendor system or a poorly secured third-party connection can serve as an entry point for attackers. Segmentation ensures that third-party access is restricted to only the necessary systems, reducing the risk of supply chain attacks. Organizations should evaluate vendor access permissions as part of their risk management strategy, ensuring that segmentation controls minimize exposure to external threats.

Business continuity and disaster recovery planning benefit from network segmentation by ensuring that critical systems remain operational during a security incident. Risk management strategies must account for how segmentation can prevent cascading failures when a breach occurs. If a ransomware attack encrypts data in one segment, proper segmentation prevents it from spreading to backup systems, cloud storage, or other essential business applications. Organizations should conduct risk assessments to determine which segments require additional redundancy, backup mechanisms, and failover strategies to ensure business continuity.

Cloud security introduces additional segmentation challenges that must be addressed within a risk management framework. Cloud environments are highly dynamic, with workloads frequently scaling up and down, making traditional segmentation methods less effective. Identity-based segmentation, software-defined networking (SDN), and cloud-native security controls help organizations enforce segmentation policies in cloud and hybrid environments. Risk assessments should consider how cloud workloads communicate, ensuring that segmentation policies prevent unauthorized access while maintaining application performance and availability.

Cyber threat intelligence enhances risk management by providing real-time insights into emerging threats, vulnerabilities, and attack trends. Organizations can use threat intelligence to refine segmentation policies based on known attack techniques and adversary behaviors. By analyzing threat intelligence data, security teams can proactively adjust segmentation rules to defend against the latest cyber threats. Automated threat intelligence integration with segmentation policies ensures that defenses remain adaptive, reducing the risk of exposure to new attack vectors.

Security monitoring and analytics play a crucial role in validating segmentation effectiveness as part of a risk management strategy. Organizations should deploy network detection and response (NDR) solutions, SIEM platforms, and endpoint monitoring tools to analyze traffic patterns, detect policy violations, and identify potential security risks. Continuous monitoring ensures that segmentation policies function as intended and provides security teams with actionable data for refining risk management practices. By integrating segmentation with monitoring capabilities, organizations can detect security incidents early and respond before they escalate into significant breaches.

Risk management also includes evaluating the human element in cybersecurity. Many security breaches occur due to human error, misconfigurations, or lack of awareness regarding segmentation policies. Organizations must provide training and awareness programs to educate employees, IT administrators, and security teams on the importance of segmentation and how it aligns with risk management objectives. Security teams should also conduct segmentation audits and penetration tests to assess whether employees follow segmentation policies correctly and whether additional training is needed.

Incident response planning must align with segmentation strategies to ensure rapid containment and recovery from security breaches. Risk management frameworks should define how segmentation policies facilitate incident response, including predefined workflows for isolating compromised segments, restoring affected systems, and investigating security incidents. Automated response mechanisms should be integrated with segmentation controls, allowing security teams to quickly contain threats and prevent attackers from exploiting segmentation gaps. Regular incident response drills and simulations should be conducted to validate the effectiveness of segmentation policies in mitigating risk.

Organizations that integrate network segmentation into their risk management strategy benefit from improved security, reduced attack surfaces, and enhanced compliance with industry regulations. By continuously assessing risks, refining segmentation policies, and leveraging monitoring tools, businesses can proactively defend against cyber threats while maintaining operational resilience. Network segmentation is not just a technical control; it is a strategic risk management tool that helps organizations protect their digital assets, mitigate potential security incidents, and ensure long-term cybersecurity sustainability.

Encryption and Secure Communication in Segmented Networks

Encryption and secure communication are essential components of network security, ensuring that data remains protected as it moves between different segments within an organization's infrastructure. In segmented networks, communication is restricted to predefined access rules that limit unauthorized interactions. However, even within properly segmented environments, sensitive data may still be at risk if transmitted without adequate encryption. Encryption strengthens network segmentation by securing data in transit, preventing unauthorized interception, and ensuring that sensitive information remains confidential. Organizations must integrate encryption and secure communication protocols into their segmentation strategy to protect against cyber threats, compliance violations, and data breaches.

One of the primary benefits of encryption in segmented networks is data confidentiality. When data moves between network segments, it is susceptible to interception by malicious actors if left unencrypted. Attackers who gain unauthorized access to a network segment could attempt to eavesdrop on communications, extract sensitive data, or manipulate traffic to launch further attacks. By implementing end-to-end encryption, organizations ensure that data remains protected even if it is transmitted across less secure or untrusted segments. Encryption scrambles data into an unreadable format that can only be deciphered by authorized recipients possessing the appropriate decryption keys.

Encryption also plays a critical role in securing remote access to segmented networks. Many organizations implement network segmentation to protect critical assets while still allowing remote employees, third-party vendors, and cloud-based applications to access necessary resources. Without proper encryption, remote access connections may expose sensitive data to man-in-the-middle attacks, packet sniffing, or unauthorized interception. Secure communication channels such as Virtual Private Networks (VPNs), Secure Sockets Layer (SSL)/Transport Layer Security (TLS), and Secure Shell (SSH) tunnels ensure that remote connections remain encrypted, preventing attackers from compromising data integrity during transmission.

Within a segmented network, secure communication protocols must be enforced to protect inter-segment traffic. Many organizations use software-defined networking (SDN) and microsegmentation to create granular access controls that restrict lateral movement between workloads. However, even with strong segmentation policies in place, attackers may attempt to bypass access restrictions by intercepting or manipulating network traffic. Implementing TLS encryption for internal communication between applications, databases, and cloud workloads prevents unauthorized access to sensitive data, ensuring that even if a network segment is compromised, encrypted traffic remains unreadable to attackers.

Secure communication between microsegmented workloads is particularly important in cloud environments. Cloud-based applications, virtual machines, and containerized workloads frequently exchange data across dynamic environments, making encryption a necessary security measure. Cloud providers offer built-in encryption tools such as AWS Key Management Service (KMS), Azure Disk Encryption, and Google Cloud Key Management to protect data in transit and at rest. Organizations must enforce encryption policies that require all communications between cloud workloads to use TLS, IPSec, or other secure tunneling protocols to prevent data leakage and unauthorized access.

Encryption enhances network segmentation by ensuring data integrity, preventing unauthorized modification of transmitted information. Attackers may attempt to manipulate data packets within a segmented network to inject malicious payloads, alter database records, or compromise authentication credentials. Cryptographic hashing and message authentication codes (MACs) ensure that data remains unaltered during transmission, allowing recipients to verify its authenticity. Integrity checks prevent attackers from tampering with critical transactions, financial records, or confidential communications, reinforcing segmentation controls by ensuring that only legitimate data is processed.

Public key infrastructure (PKI) plays a crucial role in managing encryption across segmented networks. PKI enables organizations to issue, manage, and revoke digital certificates that authenticate devices, users, and applications within a network. By implementing certificate-based authentication, organizations can enforce encrypted communication between network segments, ensuring that only trusted entities can exchange data. PKI-based encryption strengthens segmentation by preventing unauthorized devices from establishing communication channels with sensitive resources, reducing the risk of credential theft, spoofing, and phishing attacks.

Network encryption strategies must also consider the impact of encrypted traffic inspection. While encryption protects data confidentiality, it can also obscure malicious activity if security teams lack visibility into encrypted traffic. Attackers often exploit encrypted channels to evade detection, embedding malware in encrypted payloads or using encrypted tunnels to exfiltrate sensitive data. Organizations must deploy security solutions capable of inspecting encrypted traffic without compromising privacy or performance. TLS decryption gateways, SSL inspection proxies, and deep packet inspection (DPI) technologies enable security teams to analyze encrypted traffic for threats while maintaining compliance with encryption policies.

Regulatory compliance requires organizations to enforce encryption for securing sensitive data in segmented networks. Many regulations, including the General Data Protection Regulation (GDPR), the Health Insurance Portability and Accountability Act (HIPAA), and the Payment Card Industry Data Security Standard (PCI DSS), mandate encryption for protecting personal data, financial transactions, and healthcare records. Failure to encrypt communications within a segmented network may result in compliance violations, data breaches, and legal consequences. Organizations must ensure that encryption policies align with industry regulations, implementing encryption standards such as AES-256, RSA, and SHA-256 for securing critical assets.

Encryption key management is a crucial aspect of maintaining secure communication in segmented networks. If encryption keys are poorly managed, attackers may exploit weak key storage practices to decrypt sensitive data. Organizations must implement robust key management solutions that enforce secure key generation, rotation, and revocation. Hardware security modules (HSMs), cloud key management services (KMS), and cryptographic access controls help prevent unauthorized key access, ensuring that encrypted communications remain protected from potential security breaches.

Security monitoring and logging are essential for detecting potential threats within encrypted network segments. While encryption protects data confidentiality, security teams must still monitor network traffic for signs of suspicious activity. Encrypted network segments should be integrated with Security Information and Event Management (SIEM) systems, intrusion detection and prevention systems (IDPS), and behavior analytics platforms to detect anomalies. Log correlation and traffic analysis help security teams identify unauthorized access attempts, encryption policy violations, and potential encryption-based attacks such as SSL stripping or TLS downgrade attacks.

Organizations should conduct regular penetration testing and vulnerability assessments to evaluate the effectiveness of encryption policies within segmented networks. Security teams should test whether encryption protocols are properly enforced, whether encrypted traffic is vulnerable to downgrade attacks, and whether encryption key management practices are secure. Regular security assessments help identify weaknesses in encryption implementations, allowing organizations to refine their encryption strategies and strengthen network segmentation defenses.

Encryption and secure communication provide an additional layer of protection that enhances network segmentation by safeguarding data from unauthorized access, interception, and manipulation. By enforcing encryption policies, organizations can ensure that segmented networks remain secure against evolving cyber threats, maintain compliance with regulatory standards, and prevent data breaches. Integrating encryption with segmentation strategies strengthens overall cybersecurity posture, ensuring that sensitive data remains protected in transit and at rest across all network environments.

Role of SD-WAN in Network Segmentation

Software-defined wide area networking (SD-WAN) has emerged as a transformative technology that enhances network performance, security, and scalability. As organizations expand their distributed infrastructure across multiple locations, branch offices, cloud environments, and remote workforces, traditional WAN architectures struggle to provide efficient and secure connectivity. Network segmentation, a fundamental cybersecurity practice, becomes even more complex in these dynamic environments. SD-WAN addresses these challenges by enabling intelligent traffic routing, enforcing security policies, and integrating segmentation at the network level. By leveraging SD-WAN for network segmentation, organizations can create more secure, flexible, and resilient networks while maintaining centralized control over traffic flows and access policies.

One of the key advantages of SD-WAN in network segmentation is its ability to enforce segmentation policies dynamically. Traditional segmentation approaches rely on static configurations, such as VLANs, firewalls, and access control lists (ACLs), which require extensive manual intervention to maintain. In contrast, SD-WAN uses software-defined principles to apply segmentation policies based on business intent, application behavior, and real-time network conditions. This automation reduces the operational burden on IT teams while ensuring that segmentation policies remain consistent across all network locations. SD-WAN can dynamically route traffic between different segments based on security requirements, application priorities, and network performance metrics, optimizing both security and efficiency.

Security is a critical aspect of network segmentation, and SD-WAN enhances security by integrating with next-generation firewall (NGFW) capabilities, zero trust network access (ZTNA), and secure access service edge (SASE) frameworks. Traditional WAN architectures often route traffic through a centralized data center, creating bottlenecks and increasing latency. SD-WAN allows organizations to enforce segmentation policies at the network edge, ensuring that security controls are applied before traffic reaches critical applications or data centers. By integrating security features such as deep packet inspection, intrusion prevention, and identity-based access controls, SD-WAN enables organizations to enforce segmentation policies without compromising network performance.

SD-WAN simplifies segmentation across hybrid and multi-cloud environments. Many organizations operate workloads across on-premises data centers, public clouds, and private cloud infrastructures, making it challenging to maintain consistent segmentation policies. Traditional network segmentation methods often require complex configurations to enforce security policies across different cloud platforms. SD-WAN provides a unified management layer that enables organizations to define segmentation policies centrally and apply them across all cloud environments. This ensures that cloud workloads remain isolated from unauthorized access while maintaining seamless connectivity for legitimate traffic. SD-WAN also optimizes cloud access by dynamically selecting the best network path for cloud applications, reducing latency and improving user experience.

Branch offices and remote locations benefit significantly from SD-WAN-enabled segmentation. Traditional WAN architectures require dedicated MPLS connections to enforce segmentation between branch offices and the corporate network, leading to high costs and limited flexibility. SD-WAN replaces expensive MPLS circuits with more cost-effective broadband, LTE, or 5G connections while maintaining secure segmentation policies. SD-WAN enables branch offices to segment network traffic locally, ensuring that guest Wi-Fi, employee devices, IoT systems, and business-critical applications remain isolated from each other. This segmentation reduces the risk of security breaches while allowing IT teams to manage policies centrally from a cloud-based SD-WAN controller.

Microsegmentation, a more granular approach to network segmentation, is enhanced by SD-WAN's application-aware capabilities. Traditional segmentation methods often rely on IP-based rules, which do not account for application behavior or user identity. SD-WAN leverages application-layer intelligence to enforce segmentation policies based on real-time traffic analysis. By identifying applications and enforcing identity-based access controls, SD-WAN ensures that only authorized users and devices can communicate with specific network segments. This approach aligns with zero trust security models, where access is continuously verified based on contextual factors such as user role, device security posture, and network conditions.

Performance optimization is another key benefit of SD-WAN in segmented networks. Organizations that implement segmentation for security purposes must also ensure that network performance remains optimal for business operations. SD-WAN improves performance by using intelligent traffic routing, quality of service (QoS) policies, and real-time path selection. If a network segment experiences congestion or degradation, SD-WAN can automatically reroute traffic through the best available path while maintaining segmentation policies. This prevents security policies from negatively impacting network performance and ensures that critical applications receive the necessary bandwidth and priority.

SD-WAN enhances compliance with regulatory requirements by enforcing consistent segmentation policies across all network locations. Industries such as finance, healthcare, and government require strict segmentation controls to protect sensitive data and maintain compliance with regulations such as GDPR, HIPAA, and PCI DSS. Traditional segmentation methods may struggle to enforce compliance in distributed environments, especially when managing remote branches or cloud workloads. SD-WAN simplifies compliance by providing centralized visibility, automated policy enforcement, and audit logging. Organizations can use SD-WAN to segment payment processing networks, electronic health record systems, and other regulated environments, ensuring that compliance mandates are met without disrupting business operations.

Threat detection and response capabilities are strengthened by SD-WAN's integration with security analytics and artificial intelligence-driven monitoring tools. A segmented network must be continuously monitored to detect unauthorized access attempts, policy violations, and lateral movement by attackers. SD-WAN platforms provide real-time visibility into network traffic, enabling security teams to detect anomalies and enforce corrective actions. By integrating with SIEM (Security Information and Event Management) solutions, SD-WAN allows organizations to correlate network events with security incidents, improving the ability to respond to threats in segmented environments. Automated threat mitigation features, such as isolating compromised devices or blocking malicious traffic, further enhance segmentation security.

IoT security is another area where SD-WAN improves segmentation by providing fine-grained control over connected devices. Many organizations deploy IoT sensors, smart devices, and industrial automation systems that require network connectivity but lack built-in security controls. Traditional network segmentation may struggle to isolate IoT traffic without disrupting normal operations. SD-WAN enables organizations to create dedicated network segments for IoT devices, applying strict security policies to prevent unauthorized access. By segmenting IoT traffic and enforcing zero trust principles, SD-WAN reduces the risk of IoT-based attacks, ensuring that compromised devices cannot communicate with critical business systems.

SD-WAN simplifies the management of segmentation policies through centralized orchestration and policy automation. In traditional network environments, implementing segmentation requires manual configuration of firewalls, VLANs, and routing rules across multiple locations. SD-WAN eliminates this complexity by providing a cloud-based management console that allows administrators to define segmentation policies and apply them across the entire network. Automated policy updates ensure that segmentation remains effective even as network conditions change. This centralized approach reduces operational overhead, minimizes human errors, and ensures that security policies are consistently enforced across all network segments.

Organizations that integrate SD-WAN with network segmentation benefit from improved security, enhanced performance, and greater operational agility. By leveraging SD-WAN's dynamic traffic management, application-aware policies, and security integrations, businesses can enforce segmentation across branch offices, cloud environments, and remote workforces. SD-WAN provides a scalable and cost-effective solution for implementing network segmentation, ensuring that security policies remain effective while optimizing connectivity. As cyber threats continue to evolve, SD-WAN will play an increasingly vital role in securing segmented networks and enabling organizations to maintain control over their digital infrastructure.

Microsegmentation in 5G Networks

Microsegmentation in 5G networks is a critical security measure that enhances isolation, access control, and threat mitigation in next-generation telecommunications infrastructures. As 5G networks introduce ultra-high-speed connectivity, low-latency communications, and massive device density, traditional security models struggle to address the increasing complexity and evolving cyber threats. Microsegmentation enables fine-grained control over network traffic by enforcing security policies at the application, device, and service levels. By implementing microsegmentation in 5G environments, network operators can strengthen security, prevent unauthorized lateral movement, and protect critical infrastructure from advanced cyber threats.

One of the fundamental challenges in securing 5G networks is their highly distributed architecture. Unlike previous generations, 5G relies on software-defined networking (SDN), network function virtualization (NFV), and edge computing to support a vast number of connected devices and services. This dynamic environment increases the attack surface, requiring more advanced security measures to contain threats. Microsegmentation allows operators to create isolated network slices and enforce security policies on a per-device or per-application basis. Each segment can be tailored to specific security requirements, ensuring that only authorized entities can communicate within defined network boundaries.

5G networks introduce network slicing, a key feature that enables multiple virtual networks to operate independently on a shared physical infrastructure. Each network slice can be optimized for different use cases, such as autonomous vehicles, smart cities, industrial IoT, and ultra-reliable low-latency applications. While network slicing enhances flexibility and efficiency, it also introduces security risks if slices are not adequately isolated. Microsegmentation strengthens network slicing by ensuring that security policies restrict interactions between slices, preventing unauthorized access or cross-contamination of traffic. This is particularly important in critical applications such as healthcare and emergency response, where data confidentiality and service reliability are paramount.

The integration of microsegmentation with zero trust security models further enhances 5G network security. Traditional perimeter-based security approaches are ineffective in 5G environments, where devices, applications, and users constantly move across different network domains. Zero trust principles enforce continuous verification of identities, devices, and network activity before granting access to resources. Microsegmentation aligns with zero trust by implementing strict access control policies that limit communication between segments based on predefined security parameters. Each device or application must authenticate and be explicitly authorized before interacting with other segments, reducing the risk of credential-based attacks and unauthorized lateral movement.

The massive scale of connected devices in 5G networks, including IoT devices, smart sensors, and industrial automation systems, presents significant security challenges. Many IoT devices have limited security capabilities, making them attractive targets for attackers seeking to exploit vulnerabilities and gain network access. Microsegmentation mitigates these risks by isolating IoT traffic from core network services, preventing compromised devices from communicating with critical infrastructure. By applying security policies that restrict IoT devices to only the necessary network functions, organizations can prevent attackers from leveraging IoT devices as entry points for larger-scale attacks.

Edge computing plays a crucial role in 5G networks, bringing computing resources closer to end-users to reduce latency and improve performance. However, edge environments introduce new security concerns, as they distribute network functions across multiple locations, increasing the number of potential attack vectors. Microsegmentation secures edge computing environments by isolating workloads, enforcing policy-based access controls, and preventing unauthorized interactions between different edge services. This ensures that even if an attacker compromises an edge node, they cannot easily move laterally to other parts of the network.

The application of microsegmentation in 5G private networks is particularly valuable for enterprises deploying dedicated 5G infrastructure for industrial automation, manufacturing, and mission-critical applications. Private 5G networks enable organizations to customize network configurations, optimize bandwidth, and enforce security controls tailored to their specific operational requirements. Microsegmentation enhances security in private 5G environments by separating corporate applications, production systems, and remote user access into distinct segments. By enforcing granular security policies, organizations can prevent cyber threats from affecting critical business functions while ensuring compliance with industry regulations.

Regulatory compliance is a key driver for implementing microsegmentation in 5G networks. Many industries, including healthcare, finance, and critical infrastructure, must comply with stringent data protection and cybersecurity regulations. Regulatory frameworks such as the General Data Protection Regulation (GDPR), the National Institute of Standards and Technology (NIST) Cybersecurity Framework, and industry-specific guidelines mandate network segmentation as a security control. Microsegmentation enables 5G operators and enterprises to enforce compliance by ensuring that sensitive data is only accessible within authorized segments, preventing unauthorized data exposure and ensuring secure communication.

Threat detection and response capabilities are significantly improved by integrating microsegmentation with security analytics and artificial intelligence-driven monitoring tools. Traditional threat detection methods often struggle to identify malicious activity in highly dynamic 5G environments due to the sheer volume of network traffic. Microsegmentation reduces noise by restricting communication pathways, making it easier for security teams to detect anomalies and respond to incidents. Security Information and Event Management (SIEM) platforms, behavioral analytics, and AI-driven threat detection tools can leverage microsegmentation data to identify suspicious activity, block malicious traffic, and automate incident response actions.

Automated policy enforcement is essential for managing microsegmentation in 5G networks at scale. Given the rapid provisioning and de-provisioning of network functions, security policies must be dynamically updated to reflect changes in network topology and device activity. Policy-based orchestration platforms enable real-time enforcement of microsegmentation rules, ensuring that security controls remain effective even as network conditions evolve. AI and machine learning algorithms further enhance automation by continuously analyzing network traffic, identifying emerging threats, and adjusting segmentation policies accordingly.

Performance optimization is another important consideration when implementing microsegmentation in 5G networks. While segmentation enhances security, it must not introduce latency or degrade network performance, especially for latency-sensitive applications such as real-time video streaming, autonomous vehicles, and augmented reality services. SDN and intent-based networking (IBN) technologies optimize microsegmentation by dynamically adjusting policies based on real-time network conditions. This ensures that security enforcement does not interfere with critical service performance, maintaining the high-speed, low-latency capabilities that 5G networks are designed to deliver.

The future of microsegmentation in 5G networks will involve greater integration with artificial intelligence, blockchain for identity verification, and quantum-resistant encryption technologies. AI-driven security frameworks will enable predictive segmentation, where machine learning models proactively adjust network segmentation policies based on threat intelligence and evolving attack patterns. Blockchain-based identity management solutions will strengthen authentication mechanisms, ensuring that only trusted devices and applications can access segmented network resources. As quantum computing advances, organizations will need to adopt quantum-resistant encryption techniques to secure microsegmented communications against emerging cryptographic threats.

Organizations that implement microsegmentation in 5G networks benefit from enhanced security, reduced attack surfaces, and improved compliance with regulatory standards. By isolating workloads, enforcing strict access controls, and leveraging AI-driven automation, 5G operators and enterprises can build more resilient and secure network infrastructures. As 5G adoption accelerates, microsegmentation will remain a fundamental cybersecurity strategy, ensuring that next-generation networks can support innovative applications while maintaining robust security controls.

Automating Microsegmentation Policies

Microsegmentation is a powerful security strategy that restricts network communication between workloads, applications, and devices to enforce least-privilege access. While traditional network segmentation relies on manual configurations, automating microsegmentation policies enhances security, reduces administrative overhead, and ensures real-time enforcement of security controls. In dynamic IT environments, where workloads are constantly being created, moved, or deleted, automation is essential to maintaining effective segmentation without introducing operational bottlenecks. Organizations that implement automated microsegmentation policies benefit from improved security, increased agility, and better alignment with zero trust architectures.

One of the primary drivers for automating microsegmentation policies is the complexity of managing segmentation at scale. Large enterprises, cloud service providers, and hybrid environments operate thousands of workloads across multiple data centers and cloud platforms. Manually configuring firewall rules, access control lists, and security policies for each workload is not only time-consuming but also prone to human error. Automation eliminates the need for manual rule creation and enforcement by dynamically applying segmentation policies based on predefined security templates, workload behavior, and real-time risk assessments.

Artificial intelligence and machine learning play a critical role in automating microsegmentation. Traditional segmentation methods require administrators to define rules based on IP addresses, ports, and protocols, which may not adapt to changing network conditions. AI-driven microsegmentation solutions analyze traffic patterns, application dependencies, and user behavior to automatically generate segmentation policies. These solutions continuously learn from network activity, refining access controls based on historical data and evolving threat intelligence. By leveraging AI, organizations can implement adaptive microsegmentation policies that respond to real-time security events without requiring manual intervention.

Software-defined networking (SDN) is a key enabler of automated microsegmentation. SDN abstracts network control from underlying hardware, allowing administrators to centrally define and enforce segmentation policies across distributed environments. With SDN, microsegmentation rules can be applied dynamically as workloads scale up or down, ensuring consistent security across cloud, on-premises, and hybrid infrastructures. SDN-based automation enables fine-grained policy enforcement, ensuring that only authorized applications and devices can communicate within segmented environments. This approach reduces complexity while maintaining granular access control for modern network architectures.

Policy orchestration platforms streamline the automation of microsegmentation by providing a centralized management interface for defining, enforcing, and monitoring segmentation policies. These platforms integrate with existing security tools, identity and access management (IAM) solutions, and compliance frameworks to ensure that segmentation policies align with organizational security requirements. Automation workflows allow security teams to create predefined policy templates that automatically apply to new workloads based on role-based access controls (RBAC), application type, or compliance mandates. Policy orchestration enhances operational efficiency by enabling security teams to enforce segmentation at scale without the need for manual intervention.

Zero trust security models rely on automated microsegmentation policies to enforce continuous authentication and least-privilege access. Unlike traditional perimeter-based security models, zero trust assumes that no entity should be trusted by default, requiring continuous verification of identity and security posture before granting access. Automated microsegmentation ensures that access policies are dynamically adjusted based on real-time security telemetry, user behavior analytics, and contextual risk assessments. This adaptive approach prevents unauthorized lateral movement within the network, reducing the risk of data breaches and insider threats.

Cloud-native microsegmentation solutions leverage automation to enforce security policies in dynamic, multi-cloud environments. Cloud workloads frequently move between different cloud regions, virtual machines, and containerized environments, making static segmentation policies ineffective. Automated microsegmentation in cloud environments applies identity-based access controls, ensuring that workloads communicate securely based on predefined security groups, tags, and labels. Cloud service providers offer built-in automation tools such as AWS Security Groups, Azure Policy, and Google Cloud IAM to help organizations define and enforce microsegmentation policies without manual configurations.

Automated microsegmentation also enhances regulatory compliance by ensuring that segmentation policies meet industry-specific security requirements. Many regulatory frameworks, including GDPR, HIPAA, PCI DSS, and NIST, mandate network segmentation as a security control to protect sensitive data. Automated compliance enforcement ensures that segmentation rules are continuously monitored, updated, and audited for adherence to regulatory standards. Policy automation platforms generate compliance reports, track policy violations, and provide real-time visibility into segmentation effectiveness, reducing the risk of compliance failures and regulatory penalties.

Threat detection and response benefit significantly from automated microsegmentation policies. Security information and event management (SIEM) platforms, intrusion detection systems (IDS), and endpoint detection and response (EDR) tools integrate with automated segmentation policies to provide real-time threat intelligence. When a potential security incident is detected, automated microsegmentation can dynamically isolate compromised workloads, block malicious traffic, and restrict unauthorized access. This proactive security approach minimizes the impact of cyberattacks by containing threats before they spread across the network.

Identity-driven microsegmentation enhances automation by enforcing segmentation policies based on user authentication, device posture, and real-time risk assessments. Instead of relying on static IP addresses or VLAN configurations, identity-based microsegmentation applies security controls based on user roles, multi-factor authentication (MFA), and endpoint security status. If a user's behavior deviates from normal patterns or their device is compromised, automated microsegmentation policies can adjust access controls dynamically, ensuring that only authorized and verified users can communicate within the segmented network.

Encryption and secure communication play a vital role in automated microsegmentation, ensuring that data remains protected within segmented environments. Automated security policies enforce encryption protocols such as TLS, IPSec, and VPN tunneling to secure communication between segmented workloads. Organizations can define policies that automatically apply encryption to sensitive data transfers, preventing unauthorized interception and ensuring data integrity. Automated enforcement of encryption standards reduces the risk of misconfigurations and ensures compliance with data protection regulations.

Testing and validation of automated microsegmentation policies are critical to ensuring their effectiveness. Organizations must implement continuous security testing, penetration testing, and red teaming exercises to validate that segmentation policies function as intended. Automated security validation tools simulate attack scenarios, identify segmentation gaps, and provide recommendations for policy refinement. Continuous validation ensures that segmentation controls remain effective against evolving cyber threats while minimizing disruptions to business operations.

Organizations that implement automated microsegmentation policies gain significant advantages in security, operational efficiency, and regulatory compliance. By leveraging AI-driven analytics, SDN-based orchestration, and identity-driven access controls, businesses can enforce segmentation policies dynamically and at scale. Automated microsegmentation enhances zero trust security models, prevents lateral movement, and strengthens threat detection capabilities. As networks continue to grow in complexity, automation will remain a critical component of microsegmentation strategies, ensuring that security policies are continuously enforced, optimized, and aligned with organizational risk management objectives.

Role of Containers and Virtual Machines

Containers and virtual machines (VMs) play a crucial role in modern IT infrastructures by enabling efficient resource utilization, application portability, and scalability. These technologies have transformed the way organizations deploy, manage, and secure workloads across cloud, on-premises, and hybrid environments. While both containers and virtual machines offer significant advantages, they serve different purposes and present unique security challenges, particularly in network segmentation and microsegmentation strategies. Understanding the role of containers and VMs in network security and segmentation is essential for organizations seeking to enhance their cybersecurity posture while optimizing resource allocation.

Virtual machines are a foundational technology in cloud computing and data center operations. A virtual machine is a fully isolated instance of an operating system running on a hypervisor, which abstracts the underlying hardware and enables multiple VMs to operate on a single physical server. Each VM has its own dedicated resources, including CPU, memory, and storage, making them ideal for running traditional applications and services. Virtual machines provide strong isolation between workloads, ensuring that each instance operates independently without interfering with others. This isolation is particularly beneficial in multi-tenant environments, where different users or business units require separate computing environments.

Containers, on the other hand, are lightweight, portable units that package applications and their dependencies into a single executable environment. Unlike virtual machines, containers do not require a separate operating system for each instance; instead, they share the host operating system's kernel while maintaining isolated user spaces. This architectural difference allows containers to be more efficient, reducing overhead and enabling faster deployment compared to VMs.

161

Containers are widely used for microservices architectures, continuous integration and deployment (CI/CD) pipelines, and cloud-native applications due to their ability to start, stop, and scale rapidly.

Security and network segmentation in virtual machines rely heavily on traditional methods such as firewalls, VLANs, and access control lists (ACLs). VMs are often segmented into different network zones based on their function, ensuring that sensitive workloads remain isolated from less critical systems. Hypervisor-based segmentation allows security teams to define policies that restrict communication between VMs, preventing unauthorized access and lateral movement. Virtualization security features, such as virtual private cloud (VPC) configurations, virtual firewalls, and intrusion detection systems, further enhance segmentation controls. However, because VMs operate at the operating system level, their security is dependent on proper configuration, patch management, and access control mechanisms.

Containers introduce new challenges and opportunities for network segmentation. Since containers share the same host OS kernel, traditional segmentation methods may not be sufficient to enforce strict isolation between workloads. Container orchestration platforms like Kubernetes provide built-in networking features that allow administrators to define network policies, segment containers based on namespaces, and restrict communication between containerized applications. Kubernetes network policies enable microsegmentation within a containerized environment, ensuring that only authorized containers can communicate with specific services. This approach minimizes the attack surface and reduces the risk of unauthorized access to sensitive workloads.

One of the primary security risks associated with containers is their dynamic nature. Containers are designed to be ephemeral, meaning they can be created, destroyed, and replicated within seconds. This rapid deployment model introduces challenges in maintaining consistent security policies and enforcing segmentation rules. Automated security tools that integrate with container orchestration platforms help mitigate these risks by continuously monitoring container activity, detecting policy violations, and ensuring compliance with security best practices. Role-based access control

(RBAC) and identity and access management (IAM) solutions further enhance security by restricting user permissions and limiting access to sensitive containerized applications.

Virtual machines and containers often coexist within the same infrastructure, requiring organizations to implement segmentation strategies that account for both technologies. Hybrid environments that utilize both VMs and containers must establish unified security policies that enforce segmentation across all workloads. Software-defined networking (SDN) solutions enable organizations to create network overlays that seamlessly integrate VM and container segmentation, ensuring that security policies remain consistent across different deployment models. Security teams must adopt a holistic approach to segmentation that includes monitoring, automation, and continuous policy enforcement to address the challenges of hybrid environments.

The adoption of cloud-native architectures has further accelerated the use of containers, increasing the need for advanced segmentation and security controls. Many organizations deploy containers in multi-cloud environments, where workloads operate across different cloud providers and data centers. This distributed architecture requires security policies that extend beyond traditional perimeter-based defenses, enforcing segmentation at the application and network levels. Cloud-native security tools such as AWS Security Groups, Azure Network Security Groups, and Google Cloud Firewall provide segmentation capabilities tailored for containerized workloads, ensuring that security policies are enforced regardless of the underlying infrastructure.

Zero trust security models align well with containerized environments, emphasizing continuous verification, least-privilege access, and microsegmentation. Containers can be assigned unique identities, allowing security policies to enforce access controls based on container attributes rather than relying solely on network parameters. Identity-aware segmentation ensures that only authenticated and authorized containers can access specific services, reducing the risk of credential theft and unauthorized data exposure. Zero trust principles also mandate continuous monitoring and anomaly detection, enabling security teams to respond to threats in real time.

Virtual machines and containers both require encryption to protect data in transit and at rest. VMs typically rely on traditional encryption methods, such as full-disk encryption and VPN tunneling, to secure data exchanges between segmented environments. Containers, however, require more granular encryption approaches, including service mesh architectures that encrypt inter-container communication. Service mesh solutions like Istio and Linkerd enable organizations to implement mutual TLS (mTLS) encryption between containerized applications, ensuring that communication remains secure even within the same network segment.

Regulatory compliance mandates further drive the need for effective segmentation in virtual machines and containerized environments. Industries such as healthcare, finance, and government must adhere to strict data protection standards, requiring organizations to implement network segmentation to limit access to sensitive information. Compliance frameworks such as PCI DSS, HIPAA, and GDPR emphasize the importance of isolation between workloads, making it essential for organizations to implement microsegmentation across both VMs and containers. Automated compliance enforcement tools help organizations maintain segmentation policies, generate audit logs, and detect non-compliant activities within hybrid infrastructures.

Security monitoring and threat detection play a critical role in managing segmentation for virtual machines and containers. Security teams must implement logging and analytics tools that provide visibility into workload activity, detect anomalies, and enforce segmentation policies. Security information and event management (SIEM) platforms, endpoint detection and response (EDR) solutions, and behavioral analytics tools enhance security by identifying suspicious behavior and preventing unauthorized access. Continuous monitoring ensures that segmentation policies remain effective, adapting to evolving threats and changes in workload configurations.

The evolution of virtualization and containerization technologies has reshaped how organizations approach network segmentation and security. Virtual machines offer strong isolation for traditional applications, while containers enable rapid deployment and scalability for cloud-native workloads. Organizations must implement segmentation strategies that accommodate both technologies, ensuring consistent security policies, automation, and compliance enforcement. By integrating microsegmentation, identity-based access controls, and continuous monitoring, businesses can create a secure, scalable, and resilient infrastructure that effectively mitigates cyber threats while supporting modern application architectures.

Performance Considerations in Segmented Networks

Segmented networks provide enhanced security by isolating traffic, enforcing access controls, and limiting unauthorized communication between different parts of an IT infrastructure. While segmentation improves cybersecurity posture and compliance, it also introduces potential performance challenges that organizations must address to maintain efficient network operations. A well-designed segmented network should balance security with optimal performance, ensuring that applications, services, and users experience minimal latency, high availability, and reliable connectivity. Understanding the performance considerations in segmented networks allows organizations to optimize their network architecture while maintaining robust security controls.

One of the primary performance concerns in segmented networks is increased latency. Segmentation enforces access controls between different network zones, often requiring data packets to pass through multiple security devices such as firewalls, intrusion prevention systems (IPS), and access control mechanisms. Each inspection point adds processing overhead, potentially increasing network latency. In environments where real-time communication is critical, such as financial transactions, video conferencing, or industrial automation, excessive latency can degrade user experience and impact business operations. Organizations must carefully design segmentation policies to minimize unnecessary packet inspection and ensure that security enforcement does not introduce unacceptable delays.

Network throughput is another critical factor in segmented environments. Traditional segmentation methods, such as VLANs and subnets, can create bottlenecks if not properly managed. When multiple segments share the same physical network infrastructure, high-volume traffic between segments may overwhelm network switches, routers, or firewalls, reducing overall performance. The use of next-generation firewalls (NGFWs) and software-defined networking (SDN) solutions can help optimize traffic flow by dynamically adjusting security policies based on real-time network conditions. Organizations should also ensure that network hardware and bandwidth capacity can support segmented traffic without compromising performance.

Application performance may also be affected by network segmentation, particularly in microsegmented environments where strict access controls limit communication between workloads. Many modern applications rely on microservices architectures, where multiple services must interact seamlessly across different network segments. If segmentation rules are too restrictive, application components may experience delays or failures in establishing connections. Organizations should implement application-aware segmentation that allows necessary communication while preventing unauthorized access. Service mesh technologies, such as Istio and Linkerd, provide enhanced control over inter-service communication, optimizing performance while maintaining security.

The implementation of encryption in segmented networks can introduce performance trade-offs. Many segmentation strategies require encrypted communication between segments to ensure data confidentiality and integrity. However, encryption processes consume computational resources, potentially increasing CPU and memory utilization on network devices. SSL/TLS decryption, VPN tunnels, and encrypted microsegmentation policies must be carefully managed to prevent performance degradation. Organizations should use hardware acceleration, such as dedicated cryptographic processors, to offload encryption workloads and maintain optimal network speed. Additionally, selective encryption should be applied where necessary, avoiding unnecessary encryption overhead for low-risk data flows.

Scalability is another key consideration in segmented networks. As organizations grow, their network infrastructure must accommodate an increasing number of users, devices, applications, and cloud services. Static segmentation policies that require manual updates can hinder scalability, leading to performance inefficiencies and administrative overhead. Dynamic segmentation, enabled by SDN and intent-based networking (IBN), allows organizations to automate policy enforcement based on real-time network activity. Automated segmentation reduces the complexity of managing access controls, ensuring that network performance remains consistent as new workloads and users are added to the network.

Load balancing plays a critical role in optimizing performance within segmented environments. In distributed network architectures, traffic must be evenly distributed across available resources to prevent congestion and ensure high availability. Load balancers help manage traffic flow between network segments, directing requests to the most suitable servers or cloud instances based on real-time demand. In highly segmented environments, organizations should implement intelligent load balancing strategies that take into account security policies, bandwidth availability, and geographic location to maintain optimal performance.

Cloud and hybrid network environments present unique performance challenges in segmented architectures. Many organizations operate across multiple cloud providers, on-premises data centers, and edge computing environments, requiring consistent security and segmentation policies across different platforms. Cloud-native segmentation solutions must be optimized to support high-speed connectivity between cloud workloads without introducing unnecessary delays. Organizations should use cloud-based SD-WAN solutions to optimize network routing, reduce latency, and ensure secure communication between segmented cloud resources.

Performance monitoring is essential for identifying and resolving issues in segmented networks. Network administrators must continuously track key performance indicators (KPIs) such as latency, packet loss, bandwidth utilization, and application response times to ensure that segmentation policies do not negatively impact user experience. Network monitoring tools, including SIEM platforms, network analytics solutions, and AI-driven anomaly detection systems, provide real-time visibility into segmented traffic patterns. Proactive monitoring allows organizations to detect performance bottlenecks, optimize security policies, and adjust network configurations to maintain efficient operations.

Automated policy enforcement helps streamline performance optimization in segmented networks. Traditional segmentation methods require manual configuration of firewall rules, ACLs, and VLAN assignments, which can lead to errors, misconfigurations, and performance inefficiencies. Policy-based automation tools enable organizations to dynamically adjust segmentation rules based on user identity, device posture, and application behavior. By integrating automation into network security workflows, organizations can ensure that segmentation policies adapt to changing network conditions without negatively impacting performance.

User experience is a critical factor in network segmentation performance. Employees, customers, and remote users expect seamless access to applications and services, regardless of underlying security policies. Poorly implemented segmentation can lead to slow connections, dropped packets, or restricted access to critical business applications. Organizations should conduct user experience testing to evaluate the impact of segmentation on day-to-day operations. Implementing identity-aware segmentation, which dynamically adjusts access controls based on user roles and authentication factors, helps balance security with usability, ensuring that users can perform their tasks without unnecessary restrictions.

Redundancy and failover mechanisms must be incorporated into segmented network designs to prevent performance disruptions. If a critical network segment becomes unavailable due to hardware failure, cyberattacks, or misconfigurations, alternative communication paths should be available to maintain business continuity. High-availability architectures, including redundant firewalls, multi-path routing, and failover clustering, ensure that segmentation policies do not create single points of failure. Organizations should conduct regular testing of failover mechanisms to confirm that traffic can be rerouted seamlessly in the event of an outage.

Optimizing performance in segmented networks requires a careful balance between security enforcement and network efficiency. Organizations must continuously evaluate the impact of segmentation policies on latency, throughput, application performance, and scalability to ensure a seamless user experience. By leveraging automation, intelligent traffic management, and real-time monitoring, organizations can maintain high-performance segmented networks that provide robust security without compromising business operations.

Penetration Testing for Segmentation Effectiveness

Penetration testing is a critical component of evaluating the effectiveness of network segmentation. While segmentation is designed to limit lateral movement, restrict unauthorized access, and enhance security, misconfigurations, overlooked policies, and evolving attack techniques can create vulnerabilities. Penetration testing, often performed by ethical hackers or red teams, simulates real-world attack scenarios to identify weaknesses in segmentation controls. By systematically probing network defenses, penetration testing helps organizations validate that segmentation policies are properly enforced and capable of preventing unauthorized access to critical assets.

One of the primary objectives of penetration testing for segmentation is to assess whether security controls effectively restrict communication between network segments. In many cases, organizations implement segmentation policies but fail to verify whether they function as intended. Attackers can exploit misconfigured access control lists (ACLs), improperly segmented VLANs, or overly permissive firewall rules to bypass restrictions. Penetration testing systematically attempts to navigate these controls, testing whether an attacker can move from a low-security zone, such as a guest network or employee workstation, to a high-security segment containing sensitive databases or critical applications.

Lateral movement testing is a key focus of segmentation penetration tests. Many cyberattacks rely on lateral movement techniques to escalate privileges, exfiltrate data, or establish persistence within a network. A penetration tester will attempt to compromise an initial foothold within a low-trust segment, such as a user workstation or IoT device, and determine whether segmentation policies prevent access to higher-trust areas. Techniques such as exploiting weak credentials, abusing misconfigured remote desktop protocols (RDP), or leveraging unpatched vulnerabilities can reveal whether segmentation effectively blocks unauthorized movement. If testers can navigate between segments that should be isolated, it indicates a failure in segmentation controls.

Firewall rule validation is another essential aspect of segmentation penetration testing. Firewalls are often the primary enforcement mechanism for segmentation policies, controlling which traffic is permitted between network segments. However, complex firewall rule sets, overlapping policies, and misconfigurations can inadvertently allow unauthorized communication. Penetration testers analyze firewall rules to identify inconsistencies, test for open ports that should be restricted, and determine whether traffic filtering functions as expected. Unnecessary open ports or improperly configured rules can create pathways for attackers to bypass segmentation, making firewall validation a critical part of the testing process.

Zero trust verification is increasingly important in segmentation penetration tests. Modern security architectures adopt zero trust principles, requiring continuous verification of users, devices, and workloads before granting access. A penetration test evaluates whether zero trust policies are correctly implemented within segmented networks. This includes testing multi-factor authentication (MFA) enforcement, role-based access controls (RBAC), and microsegmentation policies that restrict communication at a granular level. If penetration testers can bypass authentication mechanisms or gain access to resources beyond their assigned permissions, it indicates weaknesses in zero trust enforcement.

Cloud and hybrid environments introduce additional complexity in segmentation testing. Many organizations operate across multiple cloud providers, each with its own security controls and network segmentation mechanisms. Cloud-based penetration tests assess whether segmentation policies are consistently enforced across different platforms, preventing unauthorized access between cloud workloads. Security groups, virtual private networks (VPNs), and cloud-native firewall rules must be tested to ensure that segmentation remains effective regardless of workload placement. Testing in hybrid environments also involves evaluating connectivity between on-premises data centers and cloud segments to identify potential security gaps.

IoT and industrial control system (ICS) segmentation testing is essential for organizations that deploy connected devices. IoT devices often lack built-in security controls, making segmentation one of the primary defenses against cyber threats. Penetration testers evaluate whether IoT segmentation prevents unauthorized access to critical infrastructure, such as industrial sensors, smart building controls, and healthcare devices. Testing involves identifying weak communication protocols, unsecured remote access points, and potential attack vectors that could compromise segmented IoT environments. Effective segmentation ensures that even if an IoT device is breached, attackers cannot escalate their attack to critical IT or OT systems.

Automated penetration testing tools enhance the efficiency of segmentation testing by continuously scanning for policy violations, open ports, and misconfigurations. While manual testing provides deep insights into advanced attack techniques, automated tools allow for large-scale assessment of segmentation controls. Tools such as network vulnerability scanners, lateral movement simulation platforms, and breach and attack simulation (BAS) solutions help organizations validate segmentation effectiveness on an ongoing basis. By integrating automated testing with manual penetration testing, organizations gain a comprehensive view of segmentation security.

Compliance-driven penetration testing ensures that segmentation policies meet regulatory requirements. Many industries, including finance, healthcare, and critical infrastructure, must adhere to strict network segmentation guidelines to protect sensitive data. Regulations such as PCI DSS require that payment processing environments be isolated from other network segments, while HIPAA mandates segmentation to safeguard protected health information (PHI). Penetration testing evaluates whether these requirements are met by testing segmentation boundaries, identifying policy weaknesses, and providing evidence of compliance. Regular segmentation tests help organizations demonstrate adherence to regulatory standards and avoid potential fines or penalties.

Incident response readiness can also be evaluated through segmentation penetration tests. Organizations should assess how well their security teams detect and respond to segmentation breaches. Red team exercises simulate real-world attacks, testing whether security monitoring tools, such as Security Information and Event Management (SIEM) systems and Intrusion Detection Systems (IDS), detect unauthorized segmentation attempts. If penetration testers can bypass segmentation controls without triggering alerts or response actions, it indicates a gap in threat detection and incident response capabilities.

Remediation strategies following segmentation penetration tests involve addressing discovered vulnerabilities and refining segmentation policies. Security teams must prioritize identified risks, update firewall rules, patch vulnerabilities, and enforce stricter access controls based on test findings. Continuous improvement ensures that segmentation policies remain effective against evolving threats. Organizations should schedule regular penetration tests as part of their security lifecycle, adapting their segmentation strategies to emerging attack techniques and business requirements.

Organizations that conduct thorough segmentation penetration tests enhance their security posture, reduce the risk of lateral movement, and validate the effectiveness of their segmentation strategies. By proactively identifying and addressing weaknesses, penetration testing helps ensure that network segmentation provides the intended level of security while maintaining compliance and operational efficiency. Through a combination of manual testing, automated assessments, and continuous monitoring, organizations can strengthen their segmented environments against advanced cyber threats.

Reducing Lateral Movement in Networks

Lateral movement is a common attack technique used by cybercriminals to navigate through a network after gaining initial access. Attackers move from one system to another in search of valuable data, administrative privileges, or critical infrastructure components. Reducing lateral movement is essential to minimizing the impact of security breaches and preventing attackers from escalating their access within an organization's environment. Network segmentation, microsegmentation, identity-based access controls, and continuous monitoring all play crucial roles in limiting the ability of attackers to move undetected through an enterprise network.

One of the most effective strategies for reducing lateral movement is the implementation of network segmentation. Traditional flat networks allow unrestricted communication between systems, making it easier for attackers to move laterally once inside. By dividing the network into smaller, controlled segments, organizations can restrict access to only the necessary systems and users. This containment strategy ensures that even if an attacker compromises one part of the network, they cannot easily reach other critical resources. Properly configured segmentation policies enforce strict access controls between departments, applications, and sensitive data repositories, significantly limiting an attacker's mobility.

Microsegmentation enhances this approach by applying fine-grained access controls at the workload level. Unlike traditional segmentation, which focuses on broad network divisions, microsegmentation isolates individual applications, virtual machines, and cloud workloads based on predefined security policies. This prevents unauthorized communication between workloads, ensuring that only explicitly authorized interactions are allowed. Even if an attacker gains access to a low-security workload, they cannot easily move to high-value assets without triggering security controls. Implementing microsegmentation requires careful planning, as overly restrictive policies can disrupt legitimate workflows, while insufficient enforcement leaves security gaps that attackers can exploit.

Identity and access management (IAM) is another critical component in reducing lateral movement. Many attacks leverage stolen or weak credentials to gain access to multiple systems. Enforcing multi-factor authentication (MFA) ensures that even if attackers obtain a valid username and password, they cannot access additional resources without an additional verification step. Role-based access control (RBAC) and least privilege policies further limit the scope of user access, ensuring that employees, contractors, and third-party vendors can only interact with the systems necessary for their job functions. Dynamic access controls, such as just-in-time (JIT) privileged access, can further reduce risk by granting temporary permissions only when required.

Zero trust architecture (ZTA) provides a security model specifically designed to reduce lateral movement. In a zero trust environment, no entity is trusted by default, regardless of whether it is inside or outside the network perimeter. All access requests are continuously verified using contextual factors such as device health, user behavior, and location. Network traffic is monitored in real-time, and segmentation policies are dynamically enforced to ensure that access is granted on a need-to-know basis. By implementing zero trust principles, organizations create an environment where attackers cannot easily move between systems without triggering security alerts or requiring additional authentication.

Endpoint security plays a vital role in preventing lateral movement, as many attacks originate from compromised workstations, laptops, or mobile devices. Endpoint detection and response (EDR) solutions continuously monitor for suspicious activity, such as unusual login attempts, unauthorized file access, or the execution of known attack tools. When a potential compromise is detected, automated security responses can isolate the affected endpoint, preventing attackers from using it as a launching point for further movement. Additionally, enforcing strict endpoint security policies, such as application whitelisting, disabling unnecessary services, and regularly updating software, reduces the attack surface and limits an adversary's ability to exploit vulnerabilities.

Security monitoring and threat intelligence help detect and prevent lateral movement by providing real-time visibility into network traffic and user activity. Security information and event management (SIEM) platforms aggregate logs from various sources, including firewalls, authentication systems, and endpoint security tools, to detect patterns indicative of lateral movement. Behavioral analytics tools use machine learning to establish baselines of normal user behavior, flagging anomalies that may indicate credential misuse or unauthorized access attempts. By integrating SIEM with network segmentation policies, organizations can automatically trigger containment measures when a potential security breach is detected.

Network access control (NAC) is another essential layer of defense against lateral movement. NAC solutions enforce access policies based on device identity, security posture, and compliance status before allowing network connectivity. Devices that fail security checks, such as those lacking the latest updates or missing endpoint protection software, can be quarantined in restricted network zones until they meet security requirements. This prevents compromised or unauthorized devices from moving laterally within the network, reducing the likelihood of a successful attack.

The implementation of deception technology can further limit lateral movement by misleading attackers into engaging with decoy systems. Honeypots, fake credentials, and deceptive network paths create an environment where attackers unknowingly interact with traps instead of real assets. These deception techniques provide valuable intelligence about attacker tactics while slowing their progress through the network. By diverting attackers away from critical systems, organizations gain additional time to detect, analyze, and respond to security threats before they escalate.

Cloud environments introduce additional challenges in preventing lateral movement, as workloads frequently scale across multiple data centers and cloud providers. Traditional perimeter-based security models are ineffective in cloud architectures, requiring organizations to adopt identity-aware microsegmentation and software-defined networking (SDN) to enforce access controls dynamically. Cloud-native security tools, such as AWS Security Groups, Azure Network Security Groups, and Google Cloud IAM, provide granular control over network access, ensuring that only authorized services and users can interact with cloud workloads. Continuous security monitoring and automated remediation further reduce the risk of lateral movement in cloud environments.

Patch management and vulnerability remediation also play a key role in limiting lateral movement. Attackers often exploit unpatched software vulnerabilities to escalate privileges or gain access to adjacent systems. Organizations must implement a proactive vulnerability management program that includes regular patching, automated vulnerability scanning, and prioritization of critical security updates. By addressing known vulnerabilities before attackers can exploit them, organizations reduce the likelihood of unauthorized movement within the network.

Incident response planning is essential for mitigating lateral movement when a security breach occurs. Organizations must have predefined response playbooks that outline the steps for containing and eradicating threats. Automated response mechanisms, such as network isolation, privilege revocation, and forensic analysis, enable security teams to act quickly and prevent attackers from expanding their foothold. Red team exercises and penetration testing further enhance incident response readiness by simulating real-world attack scenarios and testing an organization's ability to detect and stop lateral movement.

Reducing lateral movement requires a multi-layered security strategy that combines network segmentation, identity-based access controls, endpoint security, monitoring, deception techniques, and cloud-native protections. Organizations must continuously evaluate and refine their security posture to stay ahead of evolving threats. By implementing proactive security measures, enforcing strict access policies, and leveraging automation, organizations can effectively prevent attackers from navigating through their networks, protecting critical assets and sensitive data from compromise.

Network Segmentation for Ransomware Mitigation

Ransomware is one of the most pervasive and damaging cyber threats facing organizations today. This type of malware encrypts critical data, locks users out of their systems, and demands payment for decryption keys. Ransomware attacks have targeted businesses, healthcare facilities, government agencies, and critical infrastructure, often causing widespread disruptions and financial losses. While organizations deploy various security measures to prevent and detect ransomware infections, network segmentation remains one of the most effective strategies for mitigating the impact of an attack. By isolating different parts of the network and limiting the ability of ransomware to spread, segmentation provides a powerful defense mechanism that can significantly reduce the severity of an incident.

One of the primary ways ransomware spreads is through lateral movement. Once an attacker gains initial access to a network, they attempt to escalate privileges, identify valuable data, and move across systems to maximize the impact of the attack. Without segmentation, ransomware can propagate freely across an organization's IT environment, affecting multiple departments, servers, and endpoints. Implementing segmentation helps contain the spread by creating logical barriers between different network segments, ensuring that even if one area is compromised, the attack cannot easily move to other critical systems.

A well-designed segmentation strategy divides the network into isolated zones based on security and functionality requirements. High-value assets, such as financial databases, customer records, and intellectual property repositories, should be placed in separate, restricted segments with strict access controls. End-user workstations, which are often the initial entry point for ransomware, should be isolated from critical business systems to prevent malware from gaining access to sensitive data. Additionally, organizations should create separate network segments for third-party vendors, guest Wi-Fi, and Internet of Things (IoT) devices, as these can introduce vulnerabilities that attackers exploit.

Microsegmentation takes this approach further by enforcing access controls at the workload level. Traditional segmentation methods, such as VLANs and firewalls, create broad network segments that still allow some degree of internal movement. Microsegmentation applies granular policies that define which specific applications, devices, and services can communicate with each other. This ensures that even if ransomware infects a system, it cannot reach other workloads that do not have explicit permission to communicate with it. By restricting interactions between systems based on identity and application behavior, microsegmentation significantly reduces the attack surface for ransomware.

Least-privilege access policies are essential for effective ransomware mitigation through segmentation. Many ransomware attacks leverage compromised credentials to access sensitive systems. Implementing role-based access control (RBAC) ensures that users and devices only have access to the minimum resources required for their job functions. Segmentation policies should enforce these principles by restricting access based on predefined rules, preventing unauthorized users or compromised accounts from reaching critical assets. Privileged access should be limited to secure network segments, and any administrative access should require multi-factor authentication (MFA) to prevent unauthorized escalation.

Zero trust security models align closely with network segmentation strategies for ransomware mitigation. In a zero trust environment, no system or user is implicitly trusted, and every access request is continuously verified. Network segmentation enforces zero trust principles by ensuring that even within the organization's internal network, access is granted only after authentication and policy validation. Ransomware attacks that rely on moving laterally using compromised credentials or open network paths are significantly hindered by zero trust-based segmentation, reducing the effectiveness of the attack.

Secure remote access solutions play a critical role in segmentation-based ransomware defense. Many ransomware infections originate from remote desktop protocol (RDP) exploits, phishing attacks targeting VPN credentials, or compromised cloud-based applications. Organizations must ensure that remote access to segmented networks is tightly controlled, with access restricted to specific users, devices, and times. Virtual private networks (VPNs) should be segmented to prevent broad access to internal resources, and secure access service edge (SASE) solutions should be implemented to enforce dynamic security policies for remote users.

Ransomware mitigation also requires network segmentation for backup and disaster recovery environments. Many ransomware strains specifically target backup repositories, encrypting or deleting backup data to prevent organizations from restoring their systems without paying a ransom. Backup servers and storage systems should be placed in isolated segments with strict access controls, ensuring that ransomware cannot reach or modify them. Immutable backups, air-gapped storage, and restricted network paths further enhance the resilience of backup systems, allowing organizations to recover quickly in the event of an attack.

Network monitoring and anomaly detection are crucial components of a segmented network designed for ransomware defense. Security information and event management (SIEM) solutions, network detection and response (NDR) tools, and endpoint detection and response (EDR) platforms should be configured to monitor network segments for signs of ransomware activity. Behavioral analytics can identify unusual file access patterns, large-scale encryption operations, or unauthorized attempts to communicate with critical network segments. Automated response mechanisms can immediately isolate infected segments, preventing ransomware from spreading to unaffected areas.

Incident response planning should incorporate segmentation strategies to contain ransomware outbreaks. Organizations must define response playbooks that leverage segmentation policies to quickly isolate affected segments, disable compromised user accounts, and redirect traffic to prevent further infection. Security teams should conduct regular ransomware simulations and red team exercises to test the effectiveness of segmentation policies in stopping lateral movement. These tests help identify weaknesses in segmentation enforcement and allow organizations to refine their response strategies.

Cloud environments require specialized segmentation strategies for ransomware mitigation. Many ransomware attacks now target cloud-based storage, virtual machines, and SaaS applications, making cloud segmentation essential. Organizations should implement cloud-native segmentation policies using security groups, virtual network firewalls, and identity-based access controls to prevent ransomware from spreading within cloud environments. Cloud workload protection platforms (CWPP) and cloud security posture management (CSPM) solutions help enforce segmentation policies and detect security misconfigurations that could be exploited by attackers.

Automating segmentation policies improves ransomware defense by ensuring that security controls are consistently applied across dynamic IT environments. Manual segmentation management is prone to misconfigurations and delays in policy enforcement. Automated security policy orchestration platforms allow organizations to define segmentation rules that adapt to real-time changes in network activity, user behavior, and threat intelligence. By integrating automation with security analytics, organizations can rapidly adjust segmentation policies in response to emerging ransomware threats.

Regulatory compliance frameworks emphasize network segmentation as a key security control for protecting sensitive data. Compliance standards such as PCI DSS, HIPAA, and NIST require organizations to implement segmentation policies that limit access to critical assets. Organizations that adopt segmentation for ransomware mitigation not only reduce their risk of attack but also strengthen their compliance posture. Regular security audits and penetration testing help validate the effectiveness of segmentation policies and identify areas for improvement.

By implementing network segmentation as a core strategy for ransomware mitigation, organizations create a robust defense that limits the spread of ransomware, protects critical assets, and enhances incident response capabilities. Segmentation combined with zero trust principles, continuous monitoring, and automation provides a comprehensive approach to reducing the impact of ransomware attacks and ensuring business continuity.

Future Trends in Network Segmentation and Microsegmentation

As cyber threats continue to evolve and IT environments become more complex, network segmentation and microsegmentation are undergoing significant advancements. Organizations increasingly rely on these security strategies to prevent unauthorized access, limit lateral movement, and protect critical assets. Future trends in segmentation focus on automation, artificial intelligence, identity-based controls, and integration with emerging technologies such as 5G, edge computing, and zero trust architectures. As digital transformation accelerates, segmentation strategies will become more dynamic, adaptive, and scalable to address the growing security challenges faced by enterprises, cloud providers, and critical infrastructure.

One of the most prominent trends in network segmentation is the shift toward identity-based segmentation. Traditional segmentation relies on static network attributes such as IP addresses, VLANs, and firewall rules. However, as networks become more dynamic and workloads shift between cloud environments, static segmentation models struggle to keep up. Identity-based segmentation enforces access controls based on user identity, device posture, and contextual factors rather than network location. This approach aligns with zero trust principles, ensuring that access is granted based on real-time verification rather than implicit trust. By integrating with identity and access management (IAM) solutions, organizations can enforce fine-grained segmentation policies that adapt to changes in user roles, application behavior, and security risks.

Artificial intelligence and machine learning are playing an increasingly important role in automating network segmentation and microsegmentation. Manually configuring segmentation policies for large, distributed networks is time-consuming and prone to errors. AI-driven segmentation tools analyze traffic patterns, user behavior, and threat intelligence to automatically define and enforce segmentation policies. Machine learning algorithms continuously refine segmentation rules by identifying anomalies and adjusting access controls in real time. As AI-driven security solutions become more sophisticated, organizations will rely on automated segmentation to detect and prevent unauthorized lateral movement without the need for constant manual intervention.

Cloud-native segmentation is becoming a necessity as organizations migrate workloads to multi-cloud and hybrid environments. Cloud networks differ from traditional on-premises architectures, requiring new approaches to segmentation that extend beyond perimeter-based controls. Cloud service providers offer built-in segmentation tools such as AWS Security Groups, Azure Virtual Network Security Groups, and

Google Cloud IAM policies. Future segmentation strategies will integrate these cloud-native controls with centralized security management platforms, allowing organizations to enforce consistent segmentation policies across multiple cloud providers and on-premises infrastructure. Unified cloud segmentation will improve security visibility, simplify compliance management, and reduce the risk of misconfigurations that could expose sensitive data.

Edge computing is driving new segmentation challenges and innovations. As organizations deploy edge devices, IoT sensors, and remote computing nodes, securing distributed networks becomes increasingly complex. Traditional segmentation approaches were designed for centralized data centers and corporate offices, but edge environments require decentralized security enforcement. Future segmentation models will incorporate software-defined networking (SDN) and secure access service edge (SASE) frameworks to provide real-time policy enforcement at the edge. By extending microsegmentation capabilities to edge environments, organizations can isolate IoT devices, secure remote connections, and prevent unauthorized access to critical infrastructure.

The adoption of 5G networks is accelerating the need for dynamic segmentation strategies. Unlike previous generations of wireless networks, 5G enables network slicing, which allows multiple virtual networks to run on shared physical infrastructure. Each network slice can be tailored to specific security and performance requirements, making segmentation a fundamental component of 5G security. Future segmentation strategies will integrate with 5G network slicing to ensure that security policies are enforced across different slices based on use case requirements. Enterprises deploying private 5G networks will need advanced segmentation to protect industrial IoT deployments, autonomous systems, and mission-critical applications from cyber threats.

Zero trust network segmentation is becoming a standard approach for securing modern IT environments. Traditional segmentation models often assume that traffic within a segmented network zone is inherently trusted, but this assumption creates security gaps. Zero trust segmentation eliminates implicit trust by enforcing continuous verification and least-privilege access for all connections.

182

Organizations are increasingly adopting zero trust architectures that integrate segmentation with multi-factor authentication (MFA), endpoint security, and real-time behavioral analysis. As zero trust models mature, segmentation will be tightly integrated with identity verification, device health assessments, and contextual risk analysis to prevent unauthorized access.

Security automation and orchestration will continue to advance segmentation strategies by reducing administrative overhead and improving response times to security incidents. Organizations are adopting security orchestration, automation, and response (SOAR) platforms to dynamically enforce segmentation policies based on real-time threat intelligence. Automated workflows can instantly isolate compromised workloads, update firewall rules, and restrict access based on security alerts. As cyber threats become more sophisticated, automated segmentation will play a critical role in minimizing attack impact by containing threats before they spread across the network.

Regulatory compliance and data protection requirements are driving innovations in segmentation enforcement. Industries such as finance, healthcare, and government must adhere to strict security standards that mandate network segmentation to protect sensitive data. Future segmentation solutions will incorporate built-in compliance monitoring, automated policy validation, and real-time reporting to ensure organizations meet regulatory requirements. AI-driven compliance tools will continuously analyze segmentation policies, detect violations, and recommend corrective actions to maintain compliance with frameworks such as GDPR, HIPAA, PCI DSS, and NIST.

Deception-based segmentation is emerging as a proactive security measure to detect and contain cyber threats. Instead of relying solely on traditional segmentation methods, organizations are deploying decoy systems, honeypots, and deceptive network paths within segmented environments. Attackers attempting to navigate a segmented network unknowingly interact with false targets, triggering alerts and exposing their attack techniques. Future segmentation strategies will integrate deception technology to mislead adversaries, slowing down their progress and providing security teams with valuable intelligence on emerging threats.

Enhanced visibility and monitoring are becoming essential for effective segmentation. Organizations are investing in network detection and response (NDR) solutions that provide deep visibility into segmented traffic flows. By leveraging AI-driven analytics, security teams can detect suspicious activity, policy violations, and segmentation gaps in real time. Future segmentation platforms will integrate with extended detection and response (XDR) frameworks to correlate segmentation events with broader threat intelligence, enabling faster and more accurate incident response.

Quantum-resistant segmentation is an emerging area of research as organizations prepare for advancements in quantum computing. Traditional encryption methods that protect segmented network communications may become vulnerable to quantum attacks in the future. Organizations are beginning to explore post-quantum cryptographic algorithms and quantum-safe segmentation techniques to ensure long-term security. As quantum computing evolves, segmentation strategies will need to incorporate new cryptographic standards to maintain data protection and prevent future cryptographic attacks.

As cyber threats become more advanced and IT environments grow in complexity, network segmentation and microsegmentation will continue to evolve. The future of segmentation lies in automation, identity-based controls, cloud-native enforcement, and AI-driven security analytics. Organizations must adopt adaptive segmentation strategies that integrate with zero trust architectures, support multi-cloud environments, and leverage real-time threat intelligence to protect against evolving cyber risks. By staying ahead of segmentation trends, organizations can build resilient security frameworks that prevent lateral movement, enhance compliance, and safeguard critical assets from emerging threats.

Addressing Insider Threats with Microsegmentation

Insider threats pose a significant security risk to organizations, as they involve individuals who have legitimate access to critical systems and data. Unlike external attackers, insiders already have established trust within the network, making their activities more difficult to detect and prevent. These threats can come from malicious employees, compromised user accounts, or even unintentional mistakes that expose sensitive information. Microsegmentation is a powerful security measure that can help mitigate insider threats by enforcing strict access controls, reducing lateral movement, and providing real-time visibility into suspicious behavior. By applying microsegmentation policies, organizations can limit the potential damage caused by insiders and strengthen their overall security posture.

One of the primary ways microsegmentation addresses insider threats is by enforcing the principle of least privilege. Traditional network architectures often allow broad access across different systems, enabling insiders to move freely within the network. This unrestricted access increases the risk of data exfiltration, unauthorized modifications, and privilege escalation. Microsegmentation limits access based on user roles, job functions, and contextual factors, ensuring that employees and contractors can only interact with the specific resources they need. By defining granular security policies, organizations can prevent insiders from accessing sensitive data or critical systems beyond their designated responsibilities.

Identity-based access control is a crucial component of microsegmentation for addressing insider threats. Unlike traditional segmentation methods that rely on IP addresses or static network configurations, identity-based microsegmentation enforces security policies based on user authentication, device posture, and real-time behavioral analysis. This approach ensures that even if an insider's credentials are compromised, attackers cannot easily access unauthorized segments of the network. Organizations can integrate microsegmentation with identity and access management (IAM) solutions to enforce dynamic access controls that adapt to changes in user behavior and risk levels.

Behavioral analytics and anomaly detection enhance the effectiveness of microsegmentation in preventing insider threats. Insiders often exhibit normal activity patterns, making it difficult to distinguish between legitimate and malicious actions. Advanced microsegmentation solutions incorporate machine learning and behavioral analytics to monitor user activity within segmented environments. These systems detect deviations from normal behavior, such as accessing unfamiliar systems, downloading large amounts of data, or attempting to disable security controls. By correlating real-time analytics with microsegmentation policies, security teams can identify potential insider threats before they escalate into full-scale security incidents.

Microsegmentation helps organizations prevent data exfiltration by restricting unauthorized data transfers between network segments. Insiders seeking to steal sensitive information often attempt to move data to external storage locations, cloud services, or removable media. Microsegmentation policies can block unauthorized data flows, ensuring that only approved applications and services can transmit sensitive information. Security teams can define segmentation rules that prevent file transfers between specific segments, log unusual data movement, and automatically trigger alerts when suspicious activity is detected. By limiting data exposure, organizations reduce the risk of insiders leaking confidential information to external parties.

Compromised insider accounts present another major security challenge that microsegmentation can mitigate. Attackers frequently use phishing attacks, credential stuffing, or malware to gain control of legitimate user accounts. Once compromised, these accounts can be used to navigate the network, access sensitive data, and launch further attacks. Microsegmentation limits the impact of compromised insider accounts by enforcing access restrictions based on user behavior and device posture. If an insider account suddenly attempts to access an unauthorized segment, security policies can automatically trigger an alert, require additional authentication, or isolate the account until further investigation is conducted.

Privileged user monitoring is essential for preventing insider threats in high-risk environments. System administrators, database managers, and IT personnel often have elevated access to critical systems, making them prime targets for insider threats. Microsegmentation allows organizations to apply stricter security controls to privileged accounts, ensuring that their access is continuously monitored and restricted to necessary functions. Just-in-time (JIT) privileged access controls further enhance security by granting temporary access to critical segments only when required. By implementing segmentation policies tailored to privileged users, organizations reduce the risk of unauthorized actions by insiders with administrative privileges.

Cloud security is another area where microsegmentation plays a key role in mitigating insider threats. As organizations migrate workloads to multi-cloud and hybrid environments, insider threats can exploit misconfigurations, excessive permissions, and unsecured data storage. Cloud-native microsegmentation solutions enforce security policies that restrict access based on identity, workload characteristics, and compliance requirements. By segmenting cloud applications, organizations can prevent insiders from accessing data across different cloud platforms without proper authorization. Additionally, security teams can implement cloud-specific segmentation policies that align with industry standards such as GDPR, HIPAA, and PCI DSS to ensure compliance and data protection.

Microsegmentation enhances security monitoring by providing detailed insights into network activity. Traditional security tools often struggle to differentiate between normal and suspicious activity within a flat network architecture. By segmenting the network into smaller, controlled zones, microsegmentation enables security teams to gain granular visibility into user interactions, application communications, and data flows. This improved visibility allows for faster threat detection and response, ensuring that insider threats are identified and contained before they cause significant damage.

Automated incident response is another benefit of microsegmentation in addressing insider threats. Security teams often face challenges responding to insider threats in real-time due to the complexity of detecting and containing malicious activity. Automated microsegmentation solutions can integrate with security orchestration, automation, and response (SOAR) platforms to enforce immediate containment actions. If an insider attempts to bypass segmentation policies, security automation can isolate their account, revoke access privileges, and trigger forensic analysis. This proactive approach reduces response times and minimizes the potential impact of insider-driven security incidents.

Regulatory compliance and auditability are strengthened through microsegmentation. Many industries require strict controls over insider access to sensitive data and critical systems. Regulatory frameworks such as NIST, ISO 27001, and Sarbanes-Oxley (SOX) mandate access control measures to prevent unauthorized internal activity. Microsegmentation provides organizations with the ability to enforce and document access restrictions, ensuring compliance with industry regulations. Detailed audit logs generated by microsegmentation policies help organizations track user activity, detect policy violations, and demonstrate regulatory adherence during security audits.

Microsegmentation strategies should be continuously refined to adapt to evolving insider threats. Organizations must conduct regular security assessments, red team exercises, and penetration testing to evaluate the effectiveness of segmentation policies. By simulating insider threat scenarios, security teams can identify weaknesses in segmentation enforcement and adjust policies accordingly. Continuous improvement ensures that microsegmentation remains an effective defense against emerging insider threat tactics.

Organizations that implement microsegmentation to address insider threats gain a significant advantage in controlling access, preventing unauthorized activity, and detecting malicious behavior. By enforcing identity-based controls, leveraging behavioral analytics, and automating threat response, microsegmentation provides a comprehensive security solution for mitigating the risks posed by insiders. As cyber threats continue to evolve, organizations must prioritize microsegmentation as a fundamental component of their cybersecurity strategy to protect sensitive data, maintain regulatory compliance, and reduce the potential impact of insider-driven attacks.

Microsegmentation for Secure Remote Access

Remote access has become an essential component of modern business operations, allowing employees, contractors, and third-party vendors to connect to corporate networks from any location. However, the widespread adoption of remote work has introduced new security challenges, as traditional perimeter-based defenses are no longer sufficient to protect sensitive data and critical systems. Cyber threats such as phishing attacks, credential theft, and ransomware have exploited weaknesses in remote access solutions, leading organizations to adopt more advanced security measures. Microsegmentation has emerged as a powerful approach to securing remote access by restricting lateral movement, enforcing least-privilege access, and dynamically adapting security policies based on user identity and device posture.

One of the key benefits of microsegmentation for secure remote access is its ability to enforce granular access controls. Traditional remote access solutions, such as virtual private networks (VPNs) and remote desktop protocols (RDP), often provide users with broad access to corporate networks. If an attacker compromises a remote user's credentials, they can navigate laterally within the network, potentially accessing sensitive data or launching further attacks. Microsegmentation limits this risk by creating isolated network segments that restrict access based on predefined security policies. Instead of allowing full network access, remote users can only connect to specific applications, databases, or services necessary for their job functions.

Identity-based microsegmentation enhances security by ensuring that remote access is granted based on user authentication and contextual risk factors. Unlike traditional segmentation methods that rely on IP addresses or static firewall rules, identity-based microsegmentation dynamically adjusts access policies based on real-time user verification. Multi-factor authentication (MFA), role-based access control (RBAC), and behavioral analytics help determine whether a remote user's access request aligns with normal activity patterns. If an unusual login attempt is detected, microsegmentation can enforce stricter security measures, such as requiring additional authentication steps or limiting access to non-sensitive resources.

Device security is another critical factor in microsegmentation for secure remote access. Many remote workers use personal devices or unsecured networks to connect to corporate systems, increasing the risk of malware infections and unauthorized access. Microsegmentation ensures that access policies take into account the security posture of remote devices before granting network access. Endpoint detection and response (EDR) solutions, mobile device management (MDM) tools, and zero trust network access (ZTNA) frameworks integrate with microsegmentation policies to enforce device compliance checks. If a remote device is unpatched, running unauthorized software, or exhibiting signs of compromise, access can be restricted or denied altogether.

Zero trust principles align closely with microsegmentation strategies for securing remote access. In a zero trust environment, no user or device is implicitly trusted, regardless of their location or previous authentication status. Every access request is continuously verified using contextual risk assessments, ensuring that remote users can only interact with authorized resources. Microsegmentation enforces zero trust by segmenting network traffic at the workload level, preventing unauthorized lateral movement. This ensures that even if an attacker gains access to a remote user's account, they are unable to pivot to other critical systems or execute malicious commands beyond their assigned segment.

Cloud environments introduce additional security challenges for remote access, as users frequently connect to cloud applications, SaaS platforms, and hybrid infrastructure. Traditional segmentation models designed for on-premises networks do not provide the same level of visibility and control in multi-cloud environments. Cloud-native microsegmentation solutions help organizations enforce access policies that span on-premises and cloud workloads, ensuring consistent security across distributed architectures. By integrating with cloud security controls such as AWS Security Groups, Azure Network Security Groups, and Google Cloud IAM, microsegmentation prevents unauthorized access to cloud-based applications and databases.

Secure remote access also requires continuous monitoring and threat detection to identify and mitigate potential security incidents. Microsegmentation solutions integrate with security information and event management (SIEM) platforms, network detection and response (NDR) tools, and artificial intelligence-driven behavioral analytics to detect anomalies in remote user activity. If an unusual pattern is detected, such as an employee accessing systems outside of their normal working hours or connecting from a suspicious location, security teams can take immediate action to isolate the affected user segment. Automated response mechanisms, such as revoking access, requiring additional verification, or triggering forensic investigations, enhance security while minimizing disruption to legitimate users.

Organizations must also consider third-party and contractor access when implementing microsegmentation for secure remote access. Vendors and contractors often require temporary access to specific corporate resources, but providing them with broad network access introduces significant security risks. Microsegmentation enables organizations to define short-term, tightly controlled access policies that limit third-party users to designated network segments. These policies can be automatically revoked once the third-party engagement ends, reducing the risk of lingering access permissions that could be exploited by malicious actors.

Remote access security is further enhanced by integrating microsegmentation with secure access service edge (SASE) architectures. SASE combines network security functions, such as zero trust network access (ZTNA), firewall-as-a-service (FWaaS), and cloud access security brokers (CASB), into a single framework. By leveraging SASE, organizations can enforce microsegmentation policies at the network edge, ensuring that remote users connect securely to corporate resources without exposing the internal network to unnecessary risks. SASE solutions also improve performance by optimizing traffic routing, reducing latency, and ensuring secure access to cloud applications.

Encryption plays a crucial role in microsegmentation for secure remote access by protecting data in transit. Remote users frequently connect over public or shared networks, making encrypted communication essential to prevent data interception. Microsegmentation policies enforce encryption standards such as TLS, IPSec, and VPN tunneling to ensure that all traffic between remote users and segmented network resources remains secure. Organizations should also implement mutual TLS (mTLS) authentication to verify the identity of both clients and servers before establishing encrypted connections.

Compliance and regulatory requirements further drive the need for microsegmentation in securing remote access. Many industries, including finance, healthcare, and government, require organizations to enforce strict access controls to protect sensitive data. Regulatory frameworks such as GDPR, HIPAA, and PCI DSS mandate network segmentation as a security measure to prevent unauthorized access and data breaches. Microsegmentation ensures that remote access policies align with compliance requirements by restricting access to sensitive information and maintaining detailed audit logs of user activity. Regular security audits and penetration testing help validate the effectiveness of segmentation controls and identify areas for improvement.

Automating microsegmentation policies streamlines secure remote access management by dynamically adjusting access controls based on real-time risk assessments. Organizations leveraging artificial intelligence and machine learning-driven security automation can detect potential threats and adapt segmentation rules accordingly. Automated segmentation eliminates the need for manual policy updates, reducing administrative overhead and ensuring that security controls remain effective as network conditions evolve.

Microsegmentation provides a robust security framework for enabling secure remote access while mitigating the risks associated with cyber threats, unauthorized access, and data breaches. By enforcing granular access controls, integrating identity-based authentication, leveraging zero trust principles, and continuously monitoring network activity, organizations can protect their remote workforce without compromising security or operational efficiency. As remote work continues to grow, microsegmentation will remain a fundamental security strategy for organizations seeking to balance flexibility with comprehensive security controls.

Network Segmentation in Small and Medium Businesses (SMBs)

Small and medium-sized businesses (SMBs) are increasingly becoming prime targets for cyberattacks. Many SMBs operate under the assumption that they are not attractive to cybercriminals, but in reality, their limited security budgets and lack of advanced protections make them easier to exploit. Network segmentation is one of the most effective security strategies that SMBs can implement to protect sensitive data, prevent unauthorized access, and minimize the impact of potential security breaches. While traditionally associated with large enterprises, network segmentation is equally valuable for SMBs, providing an affordable and scalable approach to improving cybersecurity resilience.

One of the primary reasons SMBs need network segmentation is to protect critical business assets from cyber threats. Without segmentation, a network is flat, meaning that once an attacker gains access to any device, they can move freely across all systems. This lack of isolation increases the risk of ransomware spreading, data breaches occurring, and insider threats going undetected. Network segmentation creates logical divisions within the IT infrastructure, separating different departments, user groups, and critical assets to prevent unauthorized movement. This reduces the likelihood of an attacker gaining full access to an entire business network.

A key aspect of network segmentation for SMBs is dividing the network into security zones based on business needs. Employees handling financial transactions, customer records, or intellectual property should be placed in restricted network segments that have stronger access controls. Guest Wi-Fi should always be isolated from internal business systems to prevent external users from accessing sensitive information. Similarly, internet-facing systems, such as web servers and customer portals, should be segmented away from internal databases and backend applications. These logical divisions ensure that different parts of the network operate independently, reducing the attack surface and improving security.

For SMBs, implementing network segmentation does not require expensive enterprise-grade security solutions. Many modern routers, firewalls, and managed switches offer built-in segmentation features, such as VLANs (Virtual Local Area Networks) and access control lists (ACLs). VLANs allow SMBs to create separate network segments without requiring additional hardware, while ACLs enforce security policies to control traffic between segments. Cloud-based firewall services also provide easy-to-configure segmentation rules, enabling SMBs to implement security controls without requiring in-house IT expertise. By leveraging these cost-effective solutions, SMBs can significantly enhance their cybersecurity posture.

Microsegmentation offers an additional layer of security by restricting access at the individual workload level. Unlike traditional segmentation, which isolates network segments based on groups of devices, microsegmentation applies policies to specific applications, servers, and endpoints. For example, an SMB that uses cloud-based storage, customer management software, and remote desktop connections can implement microsegmentation to ensure that each service is only accessible by authorized users and devices. This prevents unauthorized lateral movement, limiting the spread of malware and reducing the risk of insider threats.

One of the biggest cybersecurity risks for SMBs is the rise of ransomware attacks. Many small businesses lack the resources to recover from a ransomware infection, making prevention critical. Network segmentation significantly reduces the impact of ransomware by containing the attack within a single segment, preventing it from spreading to other systems. By segmenting workstations, servers, and backup storage, SMBs can ensure that even if an attacker compromises one segment, critical business data remains protected. Regular testing of segmentation policies and employee awareness training further strengthen this defense against ransomware.

Third-party vendors and contractors pose another security risk for SMBs. Many businesses rely on external service providers for IT support, payment processing, and supply chain operations. If a third-party system is compromised, an attacker can use it as a gateway into the SMB's network. Segmentation allows SMBs to restrict vendor access to only the necessary systems and prevent external users from navigating the entire network. Secure remote access solutions, such as VPNs with segmentation rules and zero trust network access (ZTNA), provide additional safeguards for third-party access control.

Remote work has also increased the need for network segmentation in SMB environments. Employees accessing corporate resources from home networks introduce new vulnerabilities, as personal devices and unsecured Wi-Fi connections can be exploited by cybercriminals. Segmentation ensures that remote workers connect only to designated network segments rather than the entire business network. Cloud-based security solutions with software-defined segmentation capabilities enable SMBs to enforce access controls regardless of a user's location, reducing the risk of unauthorized access from compromised home networks.

Regulatory compliance is another factor driving the adoption of network segmentation in SMBs. Many industries require businesses to implement segmentation as a security control to protect customer data, financial transactions, and personal information. For example, businesses that process credit card payments must comply with the Payment Card Industry Data Security Standard (PCI DSS), which mandates segmentation between payment processing systems and other parts of the network. Similarly, healthcare providers handling patient records must comply with HIPAA regulations, which require access controls and network segmentation to safeguard sensitive data. Implementing segmentation not only helps SMBs meet compliance requirements but also builds customer trust and reduces the risk of legal penalties.

Monitoring and visibility are essential for ensuring that segmentation policies are working effectively. SMBs should use network monitoring tools to detect unauthorized access attempts, unusual traffic patterns, and potential security breaches. Many modern firewalls and security platforms offer real-time traffic analysis, helping businesses identify segmentation policy violations before they become serious threats. Regular security assessments, penetration testing, and vulnerability scans further validate the effectiveness of segmentation controls, ensuring that policies remain up to date and aligned with evolving security threats.

Automating segmentation policies helps SMBs maintain consistent security controls without requiring constant manual intervention. Many next-generation firewalls (NGFWs) and cloud security platforms offer automated policy enforcement, dynamically adjusting access controls based on risk assessments and real-time network activity. Automated microsegmentation solutions use artificial intelligence (AI) and machine learning to analyze traffic flows and enforce security policies without human intervention. By leveraging automation, SMBs can strengthen security while minimizing the administrative burden on IT teams.

Employee awareness and training play a crucial role in supporting network segmentation efforts. SMB employees must understand the importance of segmentation and how it impacts security. Training programs should educate staff on safe computing practices, phishing awareness, and the risks of unauthorized access. Additionally, IT personnel should receive training on configuring and managing segmentation policies effectively. A well-informed workforce helps prevent accidental security breaches and ensures that employees follow best practices when accessing segmented network resources.

Network segmentation is a vital security strategy for SMBs, providing a cost-effective way to enhance cybersecurity, prevent data breaches, and mitigate ransomware attacks. By leveraging available technology, implementing best practices, and continuously monitoring segmentation policies, SMBs can protect their critical assets while maintaining business continuity. As cyber threats continue to evolve, segmentation will remain a fundamental security measure, helping SMBs reduce risk and strengthen their overall defense posture.

Evolution of Network Segmentation Technologies

Network segmentation has evolved significantly over the years, transitioning from simple physical network divisions to sophisticated, software-defined security frameworks. As cyber threats have become more advanced and IT environments more complex, segmentation technologies have adapted to address new security challenges. Modern segmentation strategies now integrate identity-based access controls, artificial intelligence, and automation to enhance security, performance, and scalability. Understanding the evolution of network segmentation technologies provides valuable insights into how organizations can effectively implement and maintain segmentation strategies to protect critical assets and prevent lateral movement of threats.

Early network segmentation methods relied primarily on physical separation. In the early days of networking, organizations implemented segmentation by deploying separate physical networks for different departments, functions, or security levels. This approach required dedicated hardware such as routers, switches, and cabling, making it expensive and difficult to scale. While physical segmentation provided strong isolation between network segments, it was inefficient for large-scale deployments, requiring significant infrastructure investment and ongoing maintenance. As networks grew in size and complexity, organizations needed more flexible and cost-effective segmentation methods.

The introduction of virtual LANs (VLANs) marked a major advancement in network segmentation. VLANs allowed organizations to create logical network segments without the need for physical separation. By configuring VLANs on network switches, IT teams could segment traffic based on departments, business functions, or security requirements. This provided greater flexibility while reducing hardware costs. VLANs also improved network performance by reducing broadcast traffic and enhancing traffic management. However, VLAN-based segmentation had limitations, particularly in environments with dynamic workloads and cloud-based applications. VLAN misconfigurations or overly permissive access policies could create security gaps, allowing attackers to bypass segmentation controls.

Firewalls and access control lists (ACLs) further improved network segmentation by enforcing security policies at the perimeter and between internal network segments. Traditional firewalls acted as gatekeepers, controlling inbound and outbound traffic based on predefined rules. Internal segmentation firewalls were introduced to provide stricter access controls between network zones, such as separating corporate IT systems from industrial control systems (ICS) or isolating financial data from general business applications. While firewalls and ACLs strengthened security, they required extensive manual configuration and were difficult to scale in complex environments with frequent network changes.

The rise of software-defined networking (SDN) transformed network segmentation by decoupling network control from physical infrastructure. SDN introduced centralized management and dynamic policy enforcement, enabling organizations to define segmentation rules based on business intent rather than static configurations. With SDN, IT teams could automate segmentation policies, dynamically adjusting access controls in response to security threats or network changes. This approach improved scalability and reduced operational overhead, making it easier to enforce segmentation across large, distributed environments. SDN-based segmentation also enhanced visibility, allowing security teams to monitor and analyze traffic flows more effectively.

Microsegmentation emerged as a critical advancement in network security, providing fine-grained access control at the workload level. Unlike traditional segmentation, which focused on network zones, microsegmentation enforced security policies for individual applications, virtual machines, and cloud workloads. This approach allowed organizations to prevent unauthorized lateral movement by ensuring that only explicitly authorized communication was permitted between workloads. Microsegmentation became essential for securing cloud environments, hybrid infrastructures, and containerized applications, where traditional network boundaries were no longer effective.

Identity-based segmentation introduced another layer of security by enforcing access controls based on user identity, device posture, and contextual risk factors. Traditional segmentation relied on IP addresses and static network attributes, making it difficult to adapt to modern security challenges such as remote work and bring-your-own-device (BYOD) policies. Identity-based segmentation leveraged integration with identity and access management (IAM) solutions to enforce dynamic access policies that adjusted in real time based on authentication, authorization, and risk assessments. This approach aligned with zero trust security models, ensuring that access was granted based on continuous verification rather than implicit trust.

Zero trust network segmentation became the next evolutionary step, combining microsegmentation, identity-based controls, and continuous monitoring to enforce least-privilege access. In zero trust architectures, every access request is evaluated in real time, with users and devices required to authenticate and validate their security posture before gaining access to resources. Zero trust segmentation eliminated the traditional notion of trusted internal networks, ensuring that security policies applied uniformly across on-premises, cloud, and remote environments. This approach reduced the risk of insider threats and credential-based attacks while improving visibility into network activity.

Cloud-native segmentation evolved to address the unique security challenges of cloud computing, multi-cloud architectures, and serverless applications. Traditional segmentation models struggled to provide consistent security across cloud environments, where workloads frequently changed and resided across multiple platforms. Cloud-native segmentation solutions integrated directly with cloud provider security controls, allowing organizations to enforce segmentation policies that spanned on-premises and cloud workloads. This approach provided seamless security across dynamic environments, ensuring that segmentation policies adapted automatically to workload changes.

Artificial intelligence (AI) and machine learning introduced automation into network segmentation, allowing security policies to be continuously refined based on real-time network activity and threat intelligence. AI-driven segmentation solutions analyzed traffic patterns, user behavior, and historical attack data to recommend or enforce segmentation policies dynamically. By leveraging AI, organizations could detect segmentation policy violations, identify misconfigurations, and respond to security threats more effectively. Automated segmentation also reduced human errors and administrative burden, improving overall security posture while maintaining operational efficiency.

The convergence of network segmentation with secure access service edge (SASE) frameworks represented another major shift in security architecture. SASE integrated network security functions such as zero trust network access (ZTNA), firewall-as-a-service (FWaaS), and cloud access security brokers (CASB) into a unified platform. By incorporating segmentation into SASE architectures, organizations could enforce security policies at the network edge, ensuring that users, devices, and applications were securely connected regardless of location. This approach improved performance, reduced latency, and enhanced security for remote workforces and cloud-based applications.

Quantum-resistant segmentation is an emerging area of research, focusing on future-proofing network security against quantum computing threats. As quantum computers develop the ability to break traditional encryption algorithms, segmentation strategies must evolve to incorporate quantum-safe cryptographic techniques. Future segmentation technologies will integrate post-quantum encryption to ensure that network traffic remains secure against advanced cryptographic attacks. Organizations are beginning to explore quantum-resistant segmentation frameworks to protect sensitive data from potential quantum-based cyber threats.

The evolution of network segmentation technologies has significantly improved security, scalability, and automation. From physical separation to AI-driven microsegmentation, segmentation strategies have continuously adapted to meet the changing cybersecurity landscape. As networks become more dynamic, cloud-centric, and distributed, segmentation will remain a fundamental security practice, ensuring that organizations can protect critical assets, prevent lateral movement, and enforce zero trust principles across all environments. The future of network segmentation will continue to integrate emerging technologies, enabling organizations to stay ahead of evolving cyber threats while maintaining operational resilience.

Building a Segmentation Roadmap for Organizations

Developing a network segmentation roadmap is a critical step for organizations looking to enhance security, optimize network performance, and comply with regulatory requirements. A well-structured roadmap provides a strategic plan for designing, implementing, and maintaining segmentation policies that align with business objectives and security best practices. Without a clear segmentation strategy, organizations may struggle with misconfigurations, operational inefficiencies, and security gaps that could be exploited by cyber threats. Building a segmentation roadmap requires careful planning, stakeholder collaboration, and continuous evaluation to ensure that security measures remain effective as business needs evolve.

The first step in building a segmentation roadmap is conducting a comprehensive assessment of the organization's current network architecture. This involves identifying all assets, data flows, user groups, applications, and external connections that interact within the network. A detailed network inventory provides visibility into how systems communicate and where security risks exist. Organizations should also assess existing segmentation controls, including firewalls, VLANs, access control lists (ACLs), and cloud security policies, to determine whether they are adequately protecting critical assets. Understanding the current state of network segmentation helps security teams identify areas for improvement and establish a baseline for future enhancements.

Defining segmentation objectives is essential for aligning security policies with business requirements. Organizations must determine what they aim to achieve with network segmentation, whether it is preventing unauthorized access, limiting lateral movement, improving regulatory compliance, or optimizing network traffic. Business-critical assets such as financial records, customer data, intellectual property, and operational technology (OT) systems should be prioritized for segmentation to ensure they are protected against cyber threats. Organizations should also consider industry-specific regulations that require network segmentation, such as PCI DSS for payment processing environments, HIPAA for healthcare data, and NIST guidelines for government agencies.

Stakeholder involvement is crucial to the success of a segmentation roadmap. IT security teams, network engineers, compliance officers, and business leaders must collaborate to define segmentation policies that balance security with operational efficiency. Business units must be consulted to ensure that segmentation does not disrupt workflows or impact productivity. Engaging application owners and cloud administrators helps prevent conflicts between segmentation policies and application dependencies. Involving all relevant stakeholders from the beginning ensures that segmentation decisions align with business priorities while maintaining strong security controls.

A risk-based approach to segmentation helps organizations allocate security resources effectively. Not all systems and data require the same level of protection, so segmentation policies should be based on risk assessments that evaluate the sensitivity of assets, the likelihood of compromise, and the potential impact of a security breach. High-risk environments, such as those handling financial transactions, should be isolated with stricter access controls, while less critical systems can have more flexible policies. Organizations should use risk assessment frameworks to categorize assets into different security zones and define access policies accordingly.

Choosing the right segmentation model depends on the organization's IT infrastructure and security needs. Traditional segmentation methods, such as VLANs and subnet-based segmentation, provide basic isolation but may not be sufficient for modern cloud environments and dynamic workloads. Microsegmentation, which enforces granular access controls at the workload level, offers stronger protection by restricting communication between individual applications and services. Identity-based segmentation integrates with authentication and authorization mechanisms to enforce policies based on user roles, device posture, and contextual risk factors. Organizations should evaluate different segmentation approaches and select the model that best aligns with their security architecture.

Developing a phased implementation plan ensures a smooth transition to segmented network environments. Organizations should avoid implementing segmentation all at once, as this can lead to operational disruptions and unforeseen security gaps. A phased approach begins with segmenting high-risk areas, such as financial databases and sensitive applications, before expanding to broader network environments. Testing segmentation policies in a controlled environment allows security teams to validate configurations and make adjustments before full deployment. Gradual implementation also helps teams gain experience with managing segmentation policies and refining enforcement mechanisms as needed.

Policy enforcement and access control mechanisms are critical components of an effective segmentation roadmap. Organizations must define clear access policies that dictate which users, devices, and applications are allowed to communicate across network segments. Least-privilege access principles should be enforced to ensure that users only have access to the resources necessary for their roles. Role-based access control (RBAC) and multi-factor authentication (MFA) add additional layers of security by verifying user identities before granting access to segmented environments. Organizations should regularly review access policies to ensure they remain aligned with security requirements and business needs.

Monitoring and visibility are essential for maintaining the effectiveness of segmentation policies. Organizations must deploy network monitoring tools that provide real-time visibility into segmented traffic, detect policy violations, and identify potential security threats. Security information and event management (SIEM) systems, intrusion detection and prevention systems (IDPS), and behavioral analytics platforms help security teams analyze network activity and respond to suspicious behavior. Continuous monitoring ensures that segmentation policies function as intended and allows for quick remediation of misconfigurations or security incidents.

Automating segmentation policies reduces administrative overhead and enhances security efficiency. Manually managing segmentation policies across large, distributed environments can be complex and time-consuming. Automated security orchestration tools enable organizations to define dynamic segmentation rules that adjust based on real-time network conditions, user behavior, and threat intelligence. Artificial intelligence (AI) and machine learning technologies further enhance automation by analyzing traffic patterns and recommending policy optimizations. Automation simplifies segmentation management, ensuring that security policies remain up to date and responsive to emerging threats.

Testing and validation are critical steps in the segmentation roadmap to ensure policies are properly enforced. Organizations should conduct penetration testing and red team exercises to simulate real-world attack scenarios and evaluate the effectiveness of segmentation controls. Security teams should attempt to bypass segmentation policies using common attack techniques, such as credential theft, lateral movement, and privilege escalation. Regular testing identifies weaknesses in segmentation enforcement and provides actionable insights for improving security controls. Organizations should incorporate segmentation validation into their security lifecycle to maintain continuous improvement.

Incident response planning must be integrated into the segmentation roadmap to ensure quick containment of security breaches. When a cyberattack occurs, organizations need predefined response protocols that leverage segmentation to isolate affected systems and prevent further damage. Automated response mechanisms can dynamically adjust segmentation policies to contain threats in real time, blocking malicious activity before it spreads. Security teams should conduct tabletop exercises and incident response drills to test their ability to respond to breaches within segmented environments. Well-defined incident response workflows improve resilience and minimize the impact of security incidents.

A long-term segmentation strategy should include ongoing optimization and adaptation to evolving security threats. Cybercriminals continuously develop new attack techniques to bypass security controls, making it essential for organizations to refine their segmentation policies regularly. Security teams should review segmentation logs, analyze security trends, and update policies based on threat intelligence and compliance changes. Engaging in continuous improvement ensures that segmentation remains effective in protecting against emerging threats while supporting business growth and innovation.

Building a segmentation roadmap requires a combination of strategic planning, risk-based decision-making, and continuous security monitoring. By defining clear objectives, engaging stakeholders, implementing phased deployments, enforcing access controls, and leveraging automation, organizations can create a robust segmentation framework that strengthens cybersecurity resilience. A well-executed segmentation roadmap enhances security, reduces the attack surface, and ensures that organizations can effectively protect their networks from evolving cyber threats.

Final Thoughts and Best Practices

Network segmentation and microsegmentation have become essential components of modern cybersecurity strategies. Organizations face an ever-evolving landscape of cyber threats, ranging from ransomware attacks and insider threats to supply chain vulnerabilities and nation-state cyber espionage. Without proper segmentation controls, networks remain vulnerable to lateral movement, unauthorized access, and large-scale data breaches. Implementing segmentation requires a well-planned approach that aligns with business objectives, security policies, and compliance requirements. By following best practices and continuously refining segmentation policies, organizations can strengthen their security posture, improve operational efficiency, and reduce risk.

One of the most important aspects of effective segmentation is the principle of least privilege. Granting users, applications, and devices only the minimum access necessary for their roles significantly reduces the attack surface. Least-privilege access prevents unauthorized movement between network segments, limiting the damage that an attacker or compromised insider can cause. Organizations should enforce strict access controls through role-based access control (RBAC), multi-factor authentication (MFA), and just-in-time (JIT) privileged access mechanisms. This ensures that segmentation policies support security without hindering legitimate business operations.

A successful segmentation strategy must be built on visibility and monitoring. Security teams cannot protect what they cannot see, making real-time network visibility crucial for enforcing segmentation policies. Organizations should deploy network monitoring tools that provide insights into data flows, access attempts, and security violations within segmented environments. Security information and event management (SIEM) platforms, network detection and response (NDR) solutions, and AI-driven analytics enhance visibility by identifying anomalies that could indicate potential breaches. Continuous monitoring enables organizations to detect and respond to segmentation violations before they escalate into critical incidents.

Automation plays a critical role in maintaining effective segmentation policies. Manually configuring and managing segmentation rules across complex IT environments is time-consuming and prone to human error. Automated segmentation tools use artificial intelligence (AI) and machine learning (ML) to dynamically adjust policies based on real-time risk assessments. Automated policy enforcement ensures that segmentation rules remain consistent across cloud, hybrid, and on-premises environments. By leveraging automation, organizations can quickly adapt to security threats, minimize misconfigurations, and reduce administrative overhead while maintaining strong segmentation controls.

Regular testing and validation of segmentation policies are necessary to ensure that security controls function as intended. Many organizations implement segmentation but fail to test whether policies effectively block unauthorized access. Penetration testing, red teaming exercises, and breach and attack simulation (BAS) tools allow security teams to evaluate the effectiveness of segmentation controls under real-world attack conditions. Testing should focus on detecting lateral movement attempts, identifying misconfigured access policies, and ensuring that segmentation policies align with regulatory compliance requirements. Organizations should integrate segmentation testing into their security lifecycle to continuously improve their defenses.

Microsegmentation enhances traditional segmentation strategies by providing granular control over workload and application communications. Unlike traditional network segmentation, which focuses on dividing broad network segments, microsegmentation enforces access controls at the individual workload level. This approach prevents unauthorized east-west traffic within the network, ensuring that even if an attacker gains access to a system, they cannot move laterally to other critical assets. Organizations implementing microsegmentation should define security policies based on application dependencies, user identities, and real-time threat intelligence to ensure that only authorized interactions occur within segmented environments.

Compliance and regulatory requirements reinforce the need for strong segmentation policies. Many industry regulations, such as PCI DSS, HIPAA, GDPR, and NIST, mandate network segmentation to protect sensitive data and enforce access controls. Organizations must align their segmentation strategies with compliance standards to avoid regulatory penalties and protect customer information. Auditing and logging all access attempts within segmented networks provide an additional layer of accountability, ensuring that security teams can track, investigate, and report any unauthorized access attempts. Compliance-driven segmentation not only meets regulatory obligations but also strengthens overall cybersecurity resilience.

Organizations should adopt a zero trust approach when implementing segmentation policies. Zero trust assumes that no user, device, or application should be implicitly trusted, requiring continuous verification before granting access to segmented resources. Integrating zero trust principles with segmentation ensures that access decisions are based on identity, device posture, and behavioral analytics rather than network location alone. Zero trust segmentation eliminates the traditional reliance on perimeter-based security models, protecting assets regardless of whether users are accessing them from internal or external networks.

Cloud and hybrid environments require adaptive segmentation strategies that account for dynamic workloads and distributed applications. Traditional segmentation models designed for static on-premises networks are insufficient in cloud-native architectures, where workloads frequently scale and shift across multiple cloud providers. Organizations must implement cloud-native segmentation policies that enforce security controls across virtual machines, containers, and microservices. Integration with cloud security solutions, such as cloud access security brokers (CASB) and software-defined perimeter (SDP) technologies, ensures that segmentation policies remain consistent across hybrid and multi-cloud environments.

Incident response planning should incorporate segmentation as a key containment strategy. When a security breach occurs, organizations must be able to quickly isolate affected segments to prevent further compromise. Automated segmentation response mechanisms can dynamically adjust firewall rules, restrict user access, and quarantine compromised devices in real-time. Security teams should conduct regular incident response drills that test segmentation policies under simulated attack scenarios. A well-prepared incident response plan ensures that segmentation policies effectively limit the impact of security breaches and facilitate rapid recovery.

Third-party and supply chain security must be considered when designing segmentation policies. Many organizations provide external vendors, contractors, and business partners with network access, increasing the risk of supply chain attacks. Segmentation policies should isolate third-party access to specific network segments, preventing vendors from accessing sensitive internal systems. Secure remote access solutions, such as virtual private networks (VPNs) with segmentation controls or zero trust network access (ZTNA), ensure that third parties only have the necessary permissions required for their business interactions. Monitoring third-party access within segmented environments helps detect and mitigate potential security risks.

Organizations should continuously evaluate and refine their segmentation strategies to keep pace with evolving threats. Cybercriminals constantly develop new techniques to bypass segmentation controls, making it essential for security teams to update policies, conduct threat modeling exercises, and stay informed on emerging attack trends. Threat intelligence feeds, AI-driven security analytics, and automated segmentation adjustments help organizations stay ahead of evolving cyber threats. By adopting a proactive security approach, organizations can ensure that segmentation remains a strong and adaptive defense against cyberattacks.

A well-implemented segmentation strategy strengthens security, improves regulatory compliance, and enhances operational resilience. Organizations that invest in robust segmentation frameworks benefit from reduced attack surfaces, improved threat detection, and faster incident containment. By enforcing least-privilege access, leveraging automation, integrating zero trust principles, and continuously monitoring segmented environments, businesses can build a strong security foundation that protects their most critical assets. Cyber threats will continue to evolve, but organizations that follow segmentation best practices will be well-positioned to defend against emerging security challenges and maintain a secure and efficient network infrastructure.